CHRISTIAN COMMITMENT

to God
and
to the world

DESCLEE COMPANY *New York - Tournai - Paris - Rome* 1965

CHRISTIAN COMMITMENT
to God
and
to the world

+

---

by Robert Guelluy
Professor at Louvain University

TRANSLATED FROM THE THIRD FRENCH EDITION
by M. Angeline Bouchard

Originally published in French by Editions CASTERMAN (Paris-Tournai, 1962) under the title *Vie de Foi et Tâches Terrestres*.

NIHIL OBSTAT

JOHN P. SULLIVAN, M. A.
Censor Deputatus

IMPRIMATUR

+ FRANCIS CARDINAL SPELLMAN
Archbishop of New York
December 10, 1964

The nihil obstat and imprimatur are official declarations that a book or pamphlet is free of doctrinal or moral error. No implication is contained therein that those who have granted the nihil obstat and imprimatur agree with the contents, opinions or statements expressed.

Library of Congress Catalog Carl Number : 65 15994

Printed in Belgium by DESCLÉE & Cie, ÉDITEURS, Tournai (Belgium).

Table of Contents

Preface

Christian commitment to God and to the world!

In this book, a man whose sacred duty keeps him in continual contact with the light of Faith expresses his fraternal concern for those whom Providence has committed to earthly tasks.

What will happen to their Faith if their work in the world seems foreign to Faith?

And how can their earthly efforts succeed if Faith ceases to permeate them with its light?

For the God of our Faith is the Creator of the universe, and the One who, by His grace, guides it toward a new creation.

These are the thoughts that brought this book into being, page by page.

* * *

As a believer and a theologian, the author has known the unending wonder of the great mystery of God the Creator and of the love that is the key to it.

Who can discover it without wanting to share it with others?

The tenor of these pages does not deceive. For all its reserve, born of the resolve to adhere strictly to theological truth, it is a work of love.

The truths it sets forth are those that man needs, without realizing it, in order to be vitally present to His God and also to the world created by God.

The difficulties discussed, whether stemming from the intoxication of conquest or the anguish of suffering, are those

8

aroused in men's hearts by contact with things of earth, thus jeopardizing their very salvation by turning them away from God.

* * *

It is a theologian's book. But within this theologian beats the heart of a man.

I take the liberty of saying this, for it is my pleasure to know him well.

‡ Gabriel-Marie Garrone
Archbishop of Toulouse

Foreword

The story of Babel and its sequel—the vocation of Abraham—are among the most decisive episodes in the Bible. The sacred text tells us that man, intoxicated by his achievements, notably the discovery of metals that enabled him to transform his habitat and therefore his way of life, dreamed of conquering earth and heaven. God did not permit this triumph of pride. He promised the universal unity the human race was seeking, but only as a gift to be accepted in the spirit of faith. In answer to the ambitions of the artisans of Babel, God called Abraham, the father of believers.

Faith, however, does not dispense men from building their world. They must still build, but with a different spirit. We must take the world in which we live seriously, without being distracted from God. We must give ourselves totally to what we do, while cleaving with all our hearts to God alone. We must be active, and yet docile in all things to God's action within us. We must want our efforts to succeed fully, while being ready to accept suffering and defeat.

May this book offer the reader useful reflections on this way of seeing and acting that is the hallmark of the believer!

PART ONE

FAITH IN GOD THE CREATOR

I   The religious import
of the dogma of creation

" We have believed the love... " (I John 4: 16)

St. John summed up Christian faith in the words: " We have believed the love that God has in our behalf. " To believe in the Christian doctrine of creation is to believe in love. It is to see love as the origin of being, to explain the world by the presence of a love. And by the same token it is to see the universe as meaningful, as the fulfillment of a magnanimous plan, the fruit of a merciful choice that willed its existence out of the superabundance of infinite Goodness.

To be a Christian is to conceive the world as a gift, to see all reality as dependent upon a benevolent vigilance. It is to explain finite being by the presence of an infinite love.

The Prime Mover of our universe is Someone, Someone who loves and, through love, gives reality to everything that exists. Inert matter subsists only because of the living consciousness that wills it. For the believer, the world is a mystery whose key is a secret of love. The universe belongs to Someone, it was made by Someone, and it is ordered to Someone.

This dynamic presence, whose fruit and sign we see in everything that exists, also explains the events of Golgotha. The world has the same origin as the Son of Mary; it stems from the same outpouring of love that gave Christ to us. Its history is inseparable from the history of Jesus.

The dogma of creation is an integral part of the dogma of the new creation. The God who creates is the God who gives Himself to His work. It was to achieve this communion that He willed the world into existence. Calvary, in revealing God's sentiments to us, tells us of the great surge of love that is the reason for the existence of the world.

Teachings on creation and teachings on God

The Creator of the world is the God of Abraham, Isaac, and Jacob, the God of Jesus Christ. The world exists in order to be the theater of a persevering will to salvation that reaches from the first Adam to the Redeemer, by way of Abraham, Isaac, and Jacob. The God who creates through love and gives His grace through love asks us to believe in the all-powerful love with which He rules the universe. Belief in the creation demands trust in the living God, just as does belief in the Redemption.

The living God depends on Himself alone in His decisions and actions. He is the God of initiative. His inspiration comes solely from His own heart, and He is obligated only to His own perfection. He alone is the explanation for His acts. When He creates, He does so freely, with a purpose in view that He Himself has determined with complete freedom and according to a plan that no outside power could impose on Him. He does not depend on the universe He fashions, any more than He depended on the military power of the Hebrews when He let them conquer the promised land by the strength of His arm. He has willed this universe as autonomously as when He chose Israel among all the peoples of the earth. The act of creation is an act of pure generosity, as gratuitous as the decision to free the people of Abraham.

The God of love decided with complete independence to create the world for which we are indebted to Him. It was out of sheer mercy that He chose to create this universe, imperfect though it be. He brought it into existence freely, by a choice that no one influenced. He is its author, and has full responsibility for it. If evil sprawls over it, it is not because He is powerless to prevent it. If He permitted deterioration of His work, He did so deliberately, reserving for Himself the right to repair, according to plans dictated solely by His benevolence, the damage that He might have refused to tolerate in the first place.

He is the one and only Master. Answerable to no one, He cannot ask anyone else to shoulder the risks that are the consequences of His work. This world, just as He made it, with free beings who could abuse His gifts, has seemed good to Him. He knew what He was doing when He consented to this adventure. And He was not defeated by His creatures' rebellion. He had means of remedying this betrayal and set them in motion in munificient fashion. He went so far as to send His Son to share our human condition, so that He might renew it.

To profess the doctrine that all things were created by one Author, by a personal God who is absolutely autonomous in His action, is to believe in the primacy of love, to place it at the beginning and end of all reality, to hold that this love is the foundation of all that exists. It is to profess an optimism whose boldness strikes a discordant note today, and which has seemed impossible in every epoch.

The great liberation that Christianity brings to men in every age is to make them realize they are loved. The great temptation of man today, as in every age, is to refuse to accept this message or to fear to take it literally because it seems too beautiful to be true. It is harder for us to accept joy than sadness. Instinctively we are less inclined to doubt bad news than good. We are more disposed to see things at their worst than to consider favorable prospects, more inclined to dread than to hope, influenced more by anticipated difficulties than by the promise of success, more impressed by defeats than victories, quicker to notice faults than qualities. It is hard for us to hold fast to the Christian message without reservation, to remain truly convinced that the world in which we live is governed by an omnipotent love, to admit wholeheartedly the good news of the Gospel according to which all suffering is overcome and, through divine mercy, can have meaning. It is hard for us to grasp the truth of this view, to remain confident that everything lies in the hands of a God of love. We must constantly fight against an egocentric impulse to be " realistic " that keeps us from taking this magnificent love seriously, that makes us think of it as a dream and not as the core of reality, the supreme reality.

We are asked to believe in a love that gives being, moment by moment, to the world in which we live, a divine love that does not hesitate before such decisions as the Incarnation and Redemption, in order to renew this fallen world. Such a love is fundamentally contrary to the scepticism we so readily profess, mistaking it for understanding, contrary to the distrust we so often mistake for wisdom.

The trust that God asks of us is certainly a reasonable attitude. Like all human trust, it is founded on reasons, but goes far beyond them. It demands spiritual health, a balanced interplay of intellect and will. Likewise, the supernatural prudence that this trust must inspire involves both circumspection and the capacity to take risks.

Rejected once? So what

Creator and creature

Let us strive to delimit more precisely the mystery of faith in God the Creator. We have just said that this faith sees the world as a work of love, that it is inseparable from our faith in redemptive love, that it is not merely the acceptance of an idea, but willingness to trust Someone, Someone whose love is altogether gratuitous and omnipotent.

The omnipotence of the personal God is one aspect of His complete liberty. He acts without compulsion from any power outside Himself, or any possibility of gain to Himself. Nor can anything outside Himself set limits to His work, for He alone can do that. Finally He acts without any interior constraint. He is totally independent of the world that He brings into being. He is totally free when He creates, because He is perfectly Himself, independent of what He creates, and because He remains as perfectly Himself in the presence of His creatures as He would be if they did not exist. His creatures cannot set up barriers against Him or shackle His autonomy. He is perfectly free because He is perfect.

Although God is unspeakably close to His works, an abyss separates Him from them because He is infinite perfection. He belongs to a different order of being; between them and Him there is a radical break in continuity. Our God is not a force diffused in nature, nor is He the first in a series of beings ordered according to degrees of greatness. There is no proportionality whatever between Him and the most perfect of His creatures. For it is impossible to compare the finite with the infinite, completely dependent beings with the One upon whom all things depend, whose existence, perfection, and power come from Himself alone.

God is as independent in His acts as in His being. He does not create by means of instruments but through the simple efficacy of His will. His word suffices to bring the real into being, His thought shapes it, His intention is creative by its very nature. The whole of reality outside Himself is dependent upon Him. He did not find pre-existing matter to mold, and He needs no exterior help in order to create. There is no intermediary between the dependence of created being and the independence of the Creator. Everything exists under His gaze, immersed in the radical subjection of those who receive everything from outside themselves. He made the world out of nothing, that is, He made it participate in what He is. He does not need the concurrence of anything outside Himself in order to create.

The creature's state is one of absolute dependence, both in its being and in its manner of being. This dependence is as total today as in the first moment of creation. The passage of time changes nothing of the condition of created being, which consists in being kept in existence through another. God alone *is* by nature, essentially, by definition, in Himself. Everything else *is*, at every moment of its existence, only through Him, by participation in His being, through His own free choice.

The notion that the existence of the world had a beginning is secondary to the notion of the continuous contingency of this existence. In conformity with the text of Genesis, the Church speaks of the beginning of the created world. She has explicitly condemned theories on the eternity of the world bound up either with the hypothesis that matter co-exists with God and independently of Him, or that matter is the result of a liberality necessary to God in order for Him to be Himself. She looks unfavorably on the notion that time had no beginning, as this view could easily truncate the dogma of the absolute dependence of all things upon God's free initiative, a unilateral and unlimited dependence that lies at the heart of the dogma of creation.

This dogma proclaims God's complete independence with regard to His decision to create, to the forms He would give His creatures, and even to the entire created universe once it had been brought into being. It also excludes any easy solution that would picture the world as coming forth from two antagonistic authors who mutually limited one another, one the principle of good and the other responsible for evil. It excludes pantheistic and emanatistic theories that confuse the finite with the infinite, or would build a bridge between the two. The dogma of creation forbids all conceptions which deny that God is a personal Being who calls the universe into existence and governs it with supreme independence, under the impetus of a completely gratuitous love.

The doctrine of creation and the sense of mystery

The Christian doctrine of creation implies the transcendence of the living God, the infinite perfection of a personal Being who is the sole Author of the world. God causes the world to exist out of the liberality of His love, with no assistance except from His own will, and no obstacles but those He freely permits. And so powerful is His will to save all His creatures that He has decreed the Incarnation.

To believe in creation is to profess belief in a mystery. Evidently it is as impossible for us to grasp what it means to create as to understand what it means to be God; to fathom God's intentions is to be equal to Him in intellect. God's activity differs as much from our human actions as He Himself differs from us. All created beings are incomparably more dependent upon their Creator than is any artifact that can subsist independently of the artisan who made it. Between God's independence of action and ours there is more than a difference of degree. It is the difference between the infinite and the finite.

Creative action is unique. It is the only action by which the object receives its very being from the agent, and not merely its mode of being. Our intellect, accustomed to compare one finite being with another, cannot clearly comprehend what it means to create. To visualize the world as created is to think of it in terms not only of its organization, but of its existence. And it means explaining this existence not by the interaction of physical causes but by an interior life, by the living God whose efficacious thought maintains this world in being and whose love constantly encompasses it.

To think of the world as created, in the Christian sense of the word, is to think of it as one of the elements in a mystery of love. It demands that we place our trust in an entirely spontaneous and all-powerful love, that we abandon ourselves to Someone whom we know to be Love, Love in its infinite perfection, asking no accounting of Him but putting our trust in His wisdom.

And yet acceptance of this mystery, so far above our intellect, presupposes the assent of the intellect. The Church has the audacity to declare that dogma and reason are in complete accord. God created us with the capacity to think, and, as He assures us in His Revelation, with the capacity to attain to Him through our faculties as rational beings. Obviously, believing is not the same as reasoning. But for the Christian, trust in God the Creator is inseparable from trust in the reason He created. Dogma invites the philosopher to search for this hidden God, who yearns to be recognized by the human mind.

A few historical notes

Through the ages the Church has had to fight to maintain her daring belief in God the Creator. She has safeguarded her dogma in the very act of clarifying it, although the wise men of every age tried to correct it—men who were wiser than they were religious, with greater capacity for reasoning than for believing.

She has had to defend herself against the temptation that persisted for so many centuries to escape the scandal of evil by inventing a kind of malevolent co-creator responsible for the miseries of earth. In the Nicene Creed we profess our belief in one God, the sole Creator of all things, visible and invisible. The *Te Deum* invites us to praise God as the Author of all things on earth or in heaven, to consider Him, with courageous thanksgiving, as the source of all reality. In 1215 the Fourth Lateran Council defined that the devil himself was created, and created good, that even his creation was the work of love. [1]

The Church has had to defend herself against many other temptations to sacrifice the transcendence of the living God: against the peril of an anthropomorphism that denied the incomprehensible mystery of God, and against the myriad forms of pantheism. Thus, the Councils that defined the Trinitarian doctrine have clearly pointed out—in proclaiming that the Word is uncreated and identical to the Father in nature—the distinction to be made between creatures and God. The Fourth Lateran Council teaches clearly that the Author of the world is the mysterious God of Scripture, the personal Being whose perfection exceeds everything we can say about Him, the Omnipotent who brought forth the universe through mercy, the One who revealed His plan of salvation to fallen man through Moses and the prophets.

In what has been called " the flood tide of 13th century Aristotelianism, " are to be found the antecedents of modern rationalism. Reacting against the enticement of the Greek conception of a universe that must necessarily exist and subject to the infrangible law of fate, the theologians of the Middle Ages energetically defended the absolute freedom of creative love. In modern times their successors have had to maintain, against the deists, the doctrine of God's vigilant and lovingly creative presence in His work.

In the 19th century, philosophy and the natural sciences were profoundly influenced by the idea of a universal becoming, and this orientation of thought was affirmed in an antireligious climate of opinion.

Idealist philosophers insisted on the " becoming " of spirit, and imprisoned it in this becoming. Metaphysical reflection was eliminated as being devoid of objective significance. The God of all perfection was replaced in men's minds by a God who creates Himself, a God immanent in spirit and seeking to find Himself through the meanders of a thought that is constantly outreaching itself. God was no longer present in the world with

---

[1] Cf. P. Charles, " Créateur des choses visibles, " *Nouvelle Revue Théologique* (1940), pp. 261-279.

the living presence of a personal God. Once more and in a new way, He was identified with the world.

Certain representatives of the positive sciences believed that God had become useless. The actual state of the world seemed to be explained by an anterior state. The existence of man, in particular, seemed explainable by that of the animal who allegedly was his ancestor. Finding a predecessor to man seemed to obviate the need of seeking man's author.

It is not our purpose to tell the history of the successes and failures of idealistic philosophy and positivism. We merely want to call to mind the teaching of the Vatican Council which took up the doctrine of the Lateran Council and clarified it. It affirmed that it was possible for human reason to discover God the Creator, took a firm stand against pantheism, and stressed that God governs by His Providence the universe He brought into being.

After this brief summary of the positions taken by the Church on the doctrine of creation, it is fitting to mention the Encyclical *Humani generis*, a document that warns against the danger of sacrificing the intransigeance of truth to the desire of seeing it accepted. It insists on the need for orthodoxy, which willingness to adapt cannot obviate. While rejecting the agnosticism of contemporary philosophies, it maintains the doctrine of the Vatican Council, namely: reason can establish the existence of a personal God; creation is the result of God's completely free initiative, whose infallible foreknowledge in governing the world is fully compatible with the liberty He gives to man. On the question of evolution, the Encyclical invites Christians to be prudent, reminding them that they must admit the immediate creation of the soul by God; it adds, on the subject of polygenism, that the hypothesis that the human race originated from a multitude of fathers cannot be reconciled with the doctrine of original sin.

The animal world and the human world

Now that we have considered creation in general, let us consider the creation of man.

Passing over the questions of original sin and polygenism, we shall merely note that the teaching of the Church, in considering all men the children of a single father, stresses their fundamental equality in a common superiority of nature over every other fleshly being.

Reason

To accept the Christian conception of man is to believe he is made to love, and thereby return God's affection with his own. The Church's interpretation of creation is completed by her interpretation of man and God's intervention in man's appearance upon earth. We shall therefore consider these views, which will complement those we have discussed thus far.

In asking ourselves what man is, our purpose will not be to establish rigorously the spirituality of the soul and the privileges that flow from it, but rather to understand the religious significance of man's spiritual nature as Christianity sees it.

The man of whom the Church speaks is not defined by his morphological characteristics. He is distinct from animals in other ways than by the capacity of his cranial cavity, the conformation of his limbs, and the perfection of his nervous system.

Nor does she define man in terms of his technical skills. True, man stands out as the only being in this world capable of producing tools and utilizing fire. While animals are often amazingly ingenious, there is a clear-cut distinction between their capacities for adaptation in a given situation and those of man. And even though man appears to be better able than animals to adapt himself to needs and opportunities in the utilization of the material world, it is not in this respect that he differs most profoundly from the brute.

To the theologian's mind, the outstanding characteristic of man, the one that places him above all purely material beings, that is most specifically human, is his capacity to take a dispassionate view of things. Man is not only aware of the usefulness of the things around him; he also makes judgments in terms of the true and the false, good and evil. He judges the objective value of a statement, the moral quality of an action. He is not a slave of the useful, but is capable of other attitudes besides concern for his own advantage. Moreover, he is not motivated solely by the attraction or repulsiveness of external stimuli. He responds to the call of moral values. He does not merely obey his impulses as a matter of necessity, he obeys his conscience.

Man is capable of dispassionate judgments and free choices with respect not only to ideas but also to persons. It is love that makes esteem and self-giving possible. Of all earth's creatures, only man has this capacity. He alone knows what it means to respect others, to appreciate personal worth, to treat his neighbor as someone, seeing a quality in him distinct and superior to any quality in things.

Man is capable of loving his brothers, and also his God. God so loved him as to give him the capacity to respond consciously and freely to His love. In the theologian's eyes, the deepest definition of man is that he is capable of receiving the Lord, of knowing and loving Him.

Man is the king of our world, which was created out of love and in order to accomplish a plan of love. And the reason he is king is not because he is the cleverest of living creatures, but because he alone is capable of loving, of responding to God's love with his own. God made all things so that they might be at the service of this privileged being, and therefore at the service of love.[1]

Man is never so completely man as when he rises above self-interest. He is never more in possession of himself and aware of himself, than when he is making disinterested judgments and when he is giving himself. The awareness of being a person grows in a child simultaneously with the aptitude for self-giving. The tiny child says " no " for a long time before he begins to say " yes. " He can resist with instinctive, almost animal force, long before he can consent to an act of generosity. He also starts out by speaking of himself in the third person, as if he were a thing, and only much later uses the word " I, " which translates his self-awareness. The capacity to say " yes " and to say " I " go hand in hand. They stem from the awakening of the intellect.

The creature endowed with consciousness, who can possess himself by realizing he is an " I, " is endowed with an interior

---

[1] We have developed these views in " L'homme ne vit pas seulement de pain, " *Revue diocésaine de Tournai*, 4 (1949), pp. 99-109, as well as in " La signification du monde matériel et la doctrine de la création, " *ibid.*, 7 (1952), pp. 49-52.

unity of his own. He is not merely a composite of aptitudes, he cannot be reduced to an agglomeration of qualities and defects. An inventory of his character traits and potentialities does not reveal all that he is. He is not an arithmetical sum. He is *someone*, he has a personal soul.

God and human births

While qualities and defects can be hereditary, consciousness, as such, is not. That by which each man is intimately and inalienably himself is not the work of other men. It is possible to act upon a man's consciousness, influence and transform it, but no man can give consciousness to another. It is possible only to help its development. Parents can transmit their aptitudes to their children, and recognize their capacities as a family heritage. But they are not the creators of their children's privilege to be conscious beings, of their irreducible unity as persons, of their innermost " I, " but rather witnesses to these things. It is through parents that consciousness makes its appearance, but they are not its authors in the fullest sense. They have been agents in an action that is beyond them, servants of the spirit and not its artisans.

Every conscious being has something of his parents in him, but he is also something new, previously non-existent. The child depends on his parents to bring him into the world, but as a person, he is linked directly to God.

Aptitudes can be transmitted, but not the use that an autonomous person will make of them. Faults and qualities are communicable, but not the " I. " Consciousness, as such, has no ancestors. The traits of a soul are subject to heredity, the soul is inseparable in life from the body it quickens, and its mode of action depends on the body to which it is united. But the soul is not hereditary. The native qualities of a soul may come to it from parents, but the soul itself comes from God. Every human birth places parents in the presence of the Creator's direct action. The human person who is their child is His work as well as theirs. They receive from Him the being they bring into the world by a power that is a divine gift.

This is the commonly accepted doctrine of the Church. The appearance of each new human being results from a very special cooperation between man and God. Spirit is not transmitted through generation. God alone can multiply consciousnesses, and this He does through the providential means of generation. However, parents cannot multiply the " I " that each of them is merely by making use of their aptitude to procreate. Collaboration between man and the Creator is exceptionally close here, since it terminates not only in a new body to be inhabited by a soul, but in a single being, at once body and spirit.

God and the appearance of the first man

The Encyclical *Humani generis* presents a similar doctrine with regard to the intervention of God in the appearance of the first man. If each human birth depends on divine action of a different sort than in the formation of a chemical body or the birth of an animal, the appearance of the first man upon earth presupposed an altogether exceptional intervention by the Creator.

Let us look into the hypothesis of evolution. Even if the appearance of man was prepared by a progressive perfecting of the animal, the fundamental difference between animals and men is so abysmal that only God could have caused it. Man is incomparably superior to every other living being on earth. Close as the first man may have been to other living creatures, he was nevertheless profoundly different from them by his capacity to make value judgments and unselfish commitments. Close as he may have been to them in his physical life, he was infinitely superior in his spiritual life. It was a solemn moment in the evolution of the world when the word " yes " was said for the first time. The appearance of man, the advent of moral consciousness, the presence in a fleshly being of the faculty for spiritual love was a tremendous leap forward in the history of life. It was a sort of theophany, a manifestation of God whose image man is. His creation was, prior to the Incarnation by which God Himself lived a man's life and experienced the thoughts

of a man's heart, the first replica of God's own generous attitudes
in a being of flesh. The creation of the first man prepared and
in a certain sense prefigured the Incarnation.

Between the possible ancestors of the first man and the
human parents of children born in our own era, there is no
common measure. Between the animal and the spiritual being
there is more than a difference of degree. There is a difference
in nature. Whatever the role of man's possible ancestors in the
appearance of consciousness, it also differs in nature from the
role of human parenthood. While parents receive from God the
child whom they do not produce alone, they collaborate with
the Creator in an act in which their human personalities have
a part. They also participate in a remote way in the formation
of those who will be born of them by preparing, through their
own behavior, the heredity of their descendants. The possible
predecessors of the first man did not know the meaning of the
free collaboration of a person in giving, and they had little to give.

When spirit appeared on earth, when a soul entered the
world for the first time, it was a culminating point in the history
of the universe. The being who came forth was amazingly new
compared to all creatures that had existed previously. It involved
the intervention of God in a way hitherto unknown on this earth.
Above and beyond this, at the very moment God breathed spirit
into flesh, He also gave man a supplemental soul. He associated
man closely to His own life through privileges we find hard to
imagine, since we are partially deprived of them. Theology
describes them as well as it can, without being able to express
their interior components, when it calls them supernatural and
preternatural gifts. The life of grace—friendship between the
God of love and the being created for love, the completion of the
spiritual creature and the transcending of the potentialities of its
nature—developed with perfect balance in this new being,
assuring spirit an astounding triumph over matter. The first
man was completely at peace with himself, with the world, and
with God.

What must have been the interior life of a human being
at once so close to God and so close to the animal kindgom,
resembling the Lord and yet anatomically akin to animals? We
have all met unpolished persons, uninitiated into the ways of

reasoning and deduction, but endowed with very keen moral sensibilities, men and women lacking intellectual culture but whose souls are extraordinarily rich. They may seem undeveloped at first sight, but their hearts contain treasures of kindness. They may be incapable of inventing anything perhaps, except ingenious ways of expressing their love. There are candid, even naïve souls, whose spiritual maturity is amazing. They may have little education, but when it comes to good and evil, when there is question of self-giving and of God, their judgment is astonishingly sound. Such may well have been our earliest ancestors, those who were the first to live on this earth as men. They were "uncultured," but their hearts were worlds in themselves. Every soul is a universe, and in the conquest of self it is possible to keep on going indefinitely. The interior of man is a world without boundaries. And how much truer this was of the new being who was man unwarped by sin, whose equilibrium had not been destroyed by the experience of evil.

Man is made for love

To accept the Christian doctrine of creation is to believe that the existence of the universe is bound up with a mystery of love. To believe, as the Church teaches us, that man is the Creator's masterpiece on this earth is to see him as depending upon love and made for love. This is what we have been trying to say in these pages. Meditation on these very simple truths can help us to understand a little better the treasures hidden in the most familiar tenets of our Faith.

II New dimensions of the world and christian thought

Observation and interpretation

We see the world with different eyes today than we would have a century ago. First of all, from the material point of view: as the result of sensational improvements in optical instruments, electronic microscopes and telescopes have opened up new fields of vision. Secondly, from the intellectual and spiritual point of view: not only do we see more now than we did a hundred years ago, we also interpret what we see very differently.

It has been proven that the intellectual evolution and religious crisis of the Renaissance were inextricably bound up, even in the smallest details, with the conditions of life as a whole during that era. The scientific discoveries of the 18th century, concerning magnetism and electrical phenomena, for example, deeply influenced the great German Romantic philosophers. In the 19th century, theories concerning the evolution of the species coincided with Marxist views on the shaping of the individual by the milieu, and with the theses of economic liberalism on the selective role of competition. Our descendants will be able to discern in the culture of our own time interactions we are now unable to see between scientific discoveries, philosophical movements, literary and artistic trends, religious thought, and so on.

Today, as in the beginning of the modern era, Christians are sometimes disconcerted by the unfurling of the unsuspected dimensions of the universe. In the day of Copernicus and Galileo, the end of geocentrism favored rationalism. For, it was argued, if the earth is far from being the physical center of the universe, is it not childish to think, as does the Christian religion, that by virtue of the Incarnation and the Redemption the earth is at the center nevertheless? In our own time, the Russians have profited by the launching of their artificial satellites to promote the cause of atheism. Even apart from such campaigns, sincere and intelligent Christians are dumbfounded by current scientific hypotheses concerning the vastness of the universe in terms of both space and time.

In a brilliant synthesis which has aroused much thought and discussion, both on the part of men of science and theologians, Father Teilhard de Chardin set out to interpret the evolution of the created world according to a view that agrees with the concepts of the positive sciences in their present state and also with the views of faith. He starts out from scientific notions, with the intention of showing how they leave paths of access open to dogmatic truths. We mention this work of a lifetime of research only to point out wherein its approach differs from the one we are using here. We, for our part, shall reflect on a few of the guideposts of faith, asking ourselves whether they are adaptable to scientific ways of thinking.

God's choices

Authentic reality is invisible. Even our daily experience convinces us of it. Our real selves are hidden. Each of us is much better and much worse than our neighbors think we are. The human meaning of each event through which we live is also beyond appearances. Every time we focus our intellects on the immediate aspect of facts we are sure to be mistaken. It is only after reflecting on factors of the doctrinal order, and not merely on the data of the positive disciplines, that we understand others and ourselves. If facts are to be grasped in all their truth, if their significance is to be unveiled, it is not enough to carefully record and catalogue them. They must put us in the presence of something beyond themselves.

Authentic reality is invisible. The Bible tells us this of the history of the world. The universe perceptible to the senses is part of a much vaster universe. God's creation has far greater dimensions than we imagine. The real history of the world

is one of warfare between good and evil, between the call of the
God of love and resistances to love.   Now the sin that is in man
comes from something beyond man; his refusal of divine grace
stems from a more fundamental refusal whose origins lie far
deeper.   The material world is inextricably involved in the
struggle for the triumph of the spirit, because man is constantly
transforming matter even while it is transforming him.   But this
struggle between man and God, which affects the visible world,
is but the echo of another struggle.   Material beings are immersed
in a spiritual universe.   Man is a puny creature compared with
the angels and demons.   The choice to which God invites him
—and which in his present state he can make only in a gradual,
partial, and precarious way—was made long ago by these spiritual
beings in a total and definitive way.   And man is still experiencing
the repercussions of that angelic choice.   He is surrounded by
the presence of the angels on the one hand, and he is vulnerable
to infernal influences on the other.

It is in this invisible universe that the combat reaches its
greatest intensity.   According to the indications of the Bible and
of Christian Tradition, there is no distinction of sex in the angelic
world; and according to traditional theological views, that is a sign
of angelic perfection.   Each human being is imperfectly a man;
each of the two complementary sexes is human only in its own
way.   The division into sexes is a way of making up for the
limitations of each of them.   And the same holds true for the
multiplication of individuals through sexual union.   Every
angel, on the contrary, is the perfect exemplar of his species, and
unique in this species.   Artistic tradition has endowed angels
with human bodies and faces, but without the characteristics
proper to a man or woman.   It usually represents angels in the
form of adolescents before puberty, and sometimes even as
winged infants.   These images certainly do not suggest a spiritual
life of such intensity and power that even the deepest and strongest
human personality would be a feeble reflection of it.   And yet
such is the life of the angels.   These are not merely creatures of the
most consummate meekness and delicacy, but spirits in full possession of themselves, living a very intense and mature interior life.

By nature the angels are superior to men in power and
perfection, as are the infernal beings.   And yet the Bible does

not present this spirit world to us as the apple of God's eye. The invisible world that explains the visible world is, in a certain respect, only the milieu in which the latter develops. One might say that it is peripheral to the visible world. It is man and his fate that hold the center of God's attention; that is why the only-begotten Son of God became man. God has given first place in His plans not to pure spirits, but to beings on the threshold of the life of the spirit, on the boundary between spirit and matter. The creature about whom God has shown the greatest concern is the one whose "Yes!" can be only a stammer whose answer —at least during the mortal life that will decide his eternity— will always be weak and wavering.

Within the human race so inferior to the angels, God fixed His gaze on one people, itself insignificant. He did not choose the great empires to be the bearers of His work of grace. He did not show predilection for the great civilizations of India or China. Instead, He chose to befriend Israel, a random agglomeration of human beings who, when they were in Egypt, were not even a distinct people but merely a few scattered handfuls of slaves. During its history, Israel has had practically no political independence or economic power, no civilization or natural boundaries of its own. It was a race, often despised, camping on the highroad that joined Egypt with Asia. The Hebrews had only one treasure: their religion. They have contributed almost nothing else to civilization.

Within this subordinate people, God chose again. He selected Moses, a man who had failed and taken to flight. He chose Saul, from the smallest family of the lowliest tribe. To overcome Goliath, He sent out an urchin, unarmed and without military training. The mother He chose for Jesus was a little peasant girl, whom the wise men of the time would certainly never have singled out. Jesus Himself chose to live under conditions that offered little prospect for human glory. He did not establish His residence in Rome, or have a high position in view. His preferences among men, too, were deceiving. He enjoyed the company of the outcasts of society. He gathered around Him men devoid of prestige. In the judgment of a successful businessman, He could well have been a man who wasted his time with people who weren't worth it.

Dare we "Avoid" People?

And God does not change His habits. Thus, during the crucial years at the beginning of the modern era, He did not look to Napoleon. To stir France out of her spiritual lethargy He chose a deserter from the Napoleonic Army, the curé of a God-forsaken place called Ars.

The devils were probably scandalized to see God love man to the point of deciding upon the Incarnation. Many Fathers of the Church have thought it was this divine plan that provoked Satan's revolt. It would have shocked the wise men of the East or the Greek philosophers to see God take such an interest in the Jews. And would not Plato and Aristotle have been horrified by the idea that God was visiting the world in the person of a Nazarene carpenter? In fact, even the leaders of the Jewish people could not reconcile themselves to this. The apostles in their turn were abashed by Jesus' attitude toward children, fearing the little ones would make Him waste His time. They forgot that the learned men of Israel judged with the same contempt His solicitude for the twelve ignorant bumpkins that they were.

To the representatives of the great civilizations of the ancient world, the Jewish people were as far removed from the center of the universe as is our planet in the minds of modern astronomers. For the leaders of Israel, David and the Virgin Mary were as insignificant, by comparaison with the essential nucleus of the chosen people, as is the earth for the scientists who scan outer space in our own day.

Finally, for anyone who has some insight into God's ways, it would be amazing and baffling if the earth were a major star in the universe. For it is characteristic of God to show predilection for what is apparently without interest.

The true destiny of the world

Now if God intended to give the best of His attention to a negligible portion of His handiwork, why did He create the vast universe of constellations? We could easily understand that He would have been obliged to make the best of the situation if He had been confronted with a pre-existing universe. But He is the Author of all things, and subject to neither error nor repentance. It follows, therefore, that everything that exists owes its existence to a single, primordial all-embracing world view. What is this view?

The Bible tells us that the world was created for man. What meaning can we see in such an affirmation today?

The first account of the origins of the world, as told in Chapter II of Genesis, is concerned solely with the origins of man. It might well have been entitled: " History of a Family." This text does not say explicitly that all things were made by God, but it shows Him to us preparing a land of plenty for the father of the human race, placing all animals at his disposal, and finally giving him a helpmeet. The center of interest here is the destiny of the human race, which, we are told, was to live with God in peaceful trust, until sin rendered the conditions of human existence tragic and perverted even the material world.

The horizons are broader, even from the first lines of Chapter I. Here the author describes God as putting the entire universe in order. Although the stars were given religious veneration in the cults of the ancient Orient, they were reduced in Genesis to the role of utilitarian objects. The Creator disposed them in such a way as to light the day and the night, and to mark the course of the seasons. The goal and crowning glory of creation is man, whom God placed on the sixth day in the domain prepared for him. God said to man: " Fill the earth, rule the animals. I give you cereals and the fruit of trees as your food; and I make the grass grow to sustain the animals." In a parallel passage in the other account, we are told that God placed man in the Garden of Eden, to cultivate and guard it.

There is a religious overtone to these two texts. The word we translate as " cultivate " signifies the service of God in other passages. The command to subdue and rule the earth calls to mind the victor's ritual of taking possession of the goods of the vanquished after a battle. God victoriously terminates His work by handing over to man His right to the spoils.

Here we have not merely a program for the rational exploitation of the world, but a plan of life with God in a universe which man is to use with religious respect. What God expects is labor similar in inspiration to that of present-day Trappists,

rather than work considered solely in terms of maximum produc-
tivity and material progress.

The account of Creation must be considered in the context
of the Bible as a whole. The point of view here is not that of the
economist or industrial psychologist, which merely admits man's
superiority over animals in methods of production. Material
goods are desirable only if they are used in a human and religious
way. God wants man to have dominion over the universe in
a truly human way. Thus understood, the use of the earth's
riches implies a renouncement of riches. Human dominion over
the world demands that man rise spiritually above material
things. St. Francis of Assisi had greater dominion over creation
than does an engineer who tames nature but whose soul is stifled
in the process and ultimately subjugated by nature.

God gave the promised land to the Jews, but asked them to
live there in detachment, to retain the spirit of their life in the
desert. God gives material goods only in support of other goods
which are essential in His eyes. He set Adam down in the
earthly paradise, but for the purpose of having him live there
in His friendship. Likewise, Jesus gave wine to the guests at
Cana, but through a miracle that was a promise of replacing the
purification of the water ritual by the wine of the Eucharist. The
guests at this wedding did not ask that much. Adam, for his
part, was more interested in the fruit of the trees than in God's
friendship.

The material world was made for man, but with a religious
purpose. It is a temple where man officiates. Work is a kind
of liturgy; material progress is one way of going to God. The
universe revealed in the accounts of creation has a "sacral"
character. It is God's domain, so ordered by Him that
man may live in it in union with Him, in His presence, service,
and love.

The material world has been placed in man's custody so that
he might at one and the same time use it and renounce it, take
an interest in it and be detached from it, be its master and behave
in it as a servant. Even from the beginning, the Creator's essential
concern was not that everything in His universe be at the service
of human comfort. When He planted the Garden of Eden, He
placed in it the tree with the forbidden fruit.

The inspired text does not reduce the religious problem, as we too often do, to the dimensions of a psychological problem, in which only the spiritual progress of the individual is at stake. These passages do not deal only with the interior personal life of man. Those who wrote them were thinking of the fate of the whole human race and even of all things. The subsequent accounts show how great a cosmic disaster sin has been. We find the same thinking in the messianic predictions of the Old Testament and in the teaching of the New Testament on the Redemption. God will one day take all His works back into His hands, and the ultimate consummation, already begun with the first coming of Christ, will be a renewal of the whole of creation. The world of reality will be restored to its true destiny when man, for whom it was made, attains his true goal.

The essential problem into which God ventured when He called forth the world is a problem of unity. Sin has fragmentized the divine work. God seeks to put it together again by reuniting it with Himself, whereas the diabolical powers seek to wrest it from Him and divide it. Some day this unity, willed from the beginning and broken by sin, will be restored around the Redeemer. Scripture tells us of this term toward which the universe is moving. It does not tell us by what paths, except to warn us that God's ways are not ours.

What will the future of the human race be? Leaping clear of the earth's boundaries, will it colonize outer space? It is estimated that man appeared on earth at least 500,000 years ago. Until the advent of man, the progress of live was apparently very slow. But since the intervention of intelligent animals, the transformation of the world has been accelerated and the cadence has become increasingly rapid. The face of the earth has changed more in fifty years than it had during the preceding thousand. Is the invasion of other planets near? Will man soon progressively occupy the whole universe? We are obviously still at the very beginning of the human adventure and should look on ourselves as the very first Christians, witnesses and agents of a spiritual evolution in which our present ways of thinking are only a point of departure. The future will evolve far more than we think. We are too much inclined to delude ourselves that we have reached the ultimate realizations, and to ensconce ourselves in

Someday our faith will be olden days!

present positions as if they were not destined to undergo serious changes.

We are part and parcel of the world in the pursuit of our destiny, and we must give it a place in our itinerary. Either we humanize it or we make it dangerous for our human condition. Our fate is bound up with what we do with the world, whether we give it meaning or divest it of all human semblance. [1] The Redemption renews the meaning of all things for man, and thus restores the unity of creation. That is the level of revealed teaching. It does not claim to set forth a cosmography, or to document us on the physical future of our earth.

The fact remains that the spectacle of the universe as we actually know it and of its evolution appears to be one of unconscionable waste. Let us put things in the best light, and suppose that life will one day be emancipated from its present limitations, and that men will some day colonize all of outer space. The fact remains that at present only the 80,000th part of the energy released by the sun benefits the earth, the remainder being wasted; only one-third of our earth consists of land, the remainder being covered by the seas, and at best only a small portion of the continents is habitable. Moreover, countless stars have been frenziedly spinning for five billion years, delapidating energy at an unimaginable rate, whereas man appeared very late. Man's sojourn on earth has been short indeed, coming after almost five billion lost years.

But this certainly agrees with what the Bible tells us of God. He wasted His time in solicitude over Abraham and in guiding Moses, while the human race was progressing elsewhere, while powerful empires developed their technology or perfected their cultures. No, God is not a methodical businessman; He is guided by His heart. When one governs an enterprise with only a financier's concerns in mind, one does not indulge in extravagances or make light of deficits. But when one is part of a family, one's actions are very different. One does not calculate as much. Mutual love leads on occasion to unwise spending; there is no

---

[1] Cf. on this subject the author's little book, *Le travail dans la vie du chrétien* (Gembloux : Duculot, 1953).

love where there isn't a touch of folly. God is love. We must expect Him to put our wisdom to rout. St. Paul has warned us of it, and without mincing words. He spoke of the folly of the cross.

The world for the Church

Besides, we must go still further and frankly face a greater scandal than that of the disproportion between the dimensions of the world and those of the human adventure. We must declare not only that the universe was created for man, but that it was created for the Church.

In the Old Testament the idea of vocation is more central than that of creation. God is first of all the One who invaded history in order to choose Himself a people upon whom to lavish His friendship and around whom He would one day unify the whole human race. Creation is part of the same movement of His love as is this call. It is akin to the work that the Most High accomplished in Israel. The crowning of this work was to be the bestowal of a benediction upon the whole earth, a benediction merely prefigured at the beginning of the world. A rabbinical aphorism declared that God had created the universe for Israel.

In the first Chapter of Genesis, the vocabulary is often the same as that used to describe the divine action in the chosen people. For the author of this text, God's initial activity already bore the marks of His intervention in the history of the chosen people. The primordial ordering of the universe was a prelude to the omnipotent interventions by which the God of Abraham would dispose the course of events with a view to His plans for Israel. St. Paul completes this line of thought when he says that all things were established in Christ and for Christ.

But if, in the eyes of the Creator, the essential was the regrouping of men in the spiritual unity of the New Israel, outward appearances effectively concealed this fact. Abraham had to wait a long time, and against all probability, for the son who would be the wellspring of the innumerable posterity promised him. Then his descendants seemed quickly forgotten by God, and their history was devoid of grandeur until the time of Moses. There followed new trials, and the prosperity of the Davidical epoch had no morrow even though it may have justified high hopes for a while. Probably the greatest disappointment, in the succession of Israel's trials, was what happened to King Josias. He was a prince according to God, a man of religion and likewise endowed with the qualities of leadership. He was looked upon as new David, and hope for redress revived. But Josias perished in 609, while a young man, confronting the Egyptian army.

This was henceforth the fate of all optimism born of hopes. Israel experienced deportation and foreign occupations. The situation was as dark as ever when Christ appeared, for Palestine was then under the Roman yoke. The hopes that the Messias stirred anew were soon dashed. Calvary followed swiftly upon the triumph of Palm Sunday.

Such has been the course of events throughout the history of the Church. God seems to take pleasure in losing the trump cards He holds in His hand. Accidents, unlucky chance, and persecutions are always ruining the most precious victories and reducing the fruit of painful effort to naught. God chooses to make a saint of a certain man, but refuses to give him intelligence or health, thus giving him little influence on others. Another has a profound influence on his time, but dies prematurely. One man would have accomplished wonders if he had had the minimum financial resources he needed, whereas another would have produced much fruit if he had had a few more friends to help him. God does not seem to be in any hurry, and His work is always being checkmated in one way or another. In one quarter the Church is the victim of misunderstanding, or of the lethargy of those who govern her; elsewhere she may be the victim of excessive zeal. Here is a priest who apparently is doing everything in his power, but unfortunately the same does not seem to be true of God who could have prevented the fire that destroyed his social service center, the disaffection of a young man on whom he relied, or the harm caused by his well-intentioned words. And the work of the Church is thwarted not only by accidents but also by the progress of civilization, while Providence seems to leave her to her own devices.

But God works even in the midst of human defeats, even if in an entirely different way than had been foreseen. And His goals are far higher. Thus the misfortunes that followed the death of King Josias led to a great revival of religious thought and to an unexpected purification of hope. The failure of Calvary was really a victory which all our crucifixes commemorate. The Church's trials force her to rekindle her faith, spiritualize her hope, and purify her charity.

That's why He first / Perfection Striving

What God desires is not the human works we shall accomplish for Him with all our hearts, but the superhuman work He will accomplish in us if we have faith. His glory will not consist in what we offer Him from our own meager resources, but what He will consumate in us if we but give our filial assent. His glory is to be our Father and to be received as such by our faithful living of the theological life. Trust is the finest homage any person can give another. That is the gift God expects of man. What He asks of us is that we answer His love with our faith.

That is why He puts us to the test, permitting the collapse of all the earthly props around us that deceived us as to our real dispositions. We thought we were living as believers, whereas we were merely enjoying the psychological comfort of men satisfied with themselves, with their achievements, and with their capacity for friendship. We imagined we were profoundly Christian, whereas our religious life was primarily a very human form of idealism. And then He asks us to consent to be part of a small flock, devoid of influence, with no reason to be proud of ourselves. He asks us to be sure of Him simply because He is God, and not because we are pleased with our success with others and over ourselves.

We must learn to offer no resistance to God's action, to seek a higher salvation than the perfect possession of our own soul and the rallying of others to the support of our efforts. We must strive to walk with God and entrust ourselves totally to His loving mercy. We must make way for Him and open our souls to an action that will supernaturally transform us.

God offers His love to man, asking in return a faith that is prolonged into hope and charity. It is this plan that explains His wastefulness. He sacrifices everything to the strengthening of the bonds of trust. He tests the believer to make his faith more genuine. He allows defeat in order to bring back to Himself those who will always be more interested in His gifts than in Him, who forget that the world they are using is the work of His hands.

The disproportions of the Redemption

What really matters in God's eyes is the freely given loyalty of His creatures on the threshold of the world of liberty. What delights Him is the fragile trust of beings who can only stammer. But must this exchange of love, to which God sacrifices everything else, be made in a climate of unknowing, and involve so much suffering, indeed, so much pain unfecundated by the life of faith? Why is something so beautiful often so terrible here on earth?

God does not create things ready-made. Even the inanimate world is in a perpetual state of becoming. Life has gradually conquered and continues to conquer the sea, the land, the air. It perfects itself at the price of heavy sacrifices in the very act of conquering. The human condition is not only a gift of God but also the fruit of His collaboration with man, demanding man's active participation as well. God's action does not set aside His creature's freedom but invites it, as in all true friendships between persons. In seeking to unite Himself to free beings, He accepts a risk. From the beginning, He consented to the possibility of the angels' rebellion and of man's defection. In accepting the consequences of sin when it occurred, He ratified them: sin had to be punished. To the believer, it is useless to try to understand the world by abstracting the sin that dwells in it. The heart of Christianity is the doctrine of the Redemption, which reveals all things to us through a mystery of sin and mercy.

God could certainly have prevented such havoc, even while respecting the liberty of His creatures. He could have preserved every human being from sin, as He did the Blessed Virgin Mary. When He created the world, with a view to His collaboration with men in the Church of Christ, and entrusted it to men, He could surely have made a more perfect adaptation of ends and means. Every day that passes, He can, without violating the liberty He is determined to respect, better adapt the work of the Church to circumstances. The exchange of liberties, within whose context His supernatural work is accomplished, could have a less mutilated appearance.

Even more baffling than the squandering of physical energy in the universe is the relentless omnipresence of suffering. Even more baffling than suffering is the apparent defeat of the Redemption. And still more baffling than the limitations of Christ's work in this world is what He suffered for it spiritually —for He measured His own defeat and wept over Jerusalem— as well as physically.

Here the waste is most incomprehensible. Why the Incarnation, why the cross? Why share human misery in this way, instead of simply eliminating it? Why this excessive will to suffer the fate of sinners integrally? Why so much shed blood, why even one drop of Jesus' blood, when God could have drawn us back to Himself without taking part in our tragedy?

Every iota of God's work bears the marks of the Redemption. If it seems to lack proportion, the same is true of our salvation by the cross. Once we accept all that is baffling about Calvary, we can accept everything else. How can we ask an accounting of the Father in the presence of Jesus, when He consented out of love to let men nail Him to a cross? How can we ask an accounting of Jesus, crucified by us and for us?

God loves us too much! Once we admit the amazing squandering of love that made Christ suffer a bloody sweat in the Garden of Olives and resulted in His death, nothing else should surprise us. The whole of God's work is made in the image of Christ, who is its purpose and its center; and it bears His marks in every detail. Jesus wasted His time for thirty years, labored almost in vain for the next three years, and finally flung His life away. This mystery is the key to everything else.

It matters little that our planet is a tiny speck in the universe, or that the space and time inhabited by man are infinitesimal in a world created for man. These are of little account compared to the essential disproportion, namely, that the Son of God willed to become what we are, lived within our human limitations, and chose to die for us. Even if we were at the center of the world's gravitation, even if man had occupied the planets and

stars from the first moment, even if the Church included everyone
on earth, the disproportion between the salvation of the human
race and what it cost the Son of God would remain as baffling as
ever.   Whatever our own greatness or that of the Church, were
they worth the death of Jesus, inasmuch as God could have
saved us without it?

It will be objected that this does not explain God's action,
that it merely tones down one scandal by juxtaposing it to a
still greater scandal.   And this is true.   We have believed in a love,
a love beyond measure.   To believe in a love is hard, it requires not
only intellect but soul.   " This is a hard saying! "   Such was the
Jews' reaction to Our Lord when He gave them a glimpse of
God's love in announcing the Eucharist.   The excessiveness of
redemptive love puts our faith to the test.   However, if we believe
in this inordinate love of the God of holiness for sinful man,
we need not be surprised by any of the disharmonies in the work
of God.

Can this sort of justification of God by recourse to the
data of faith be a valid argument for anyone but the believer?
Of course not.   But the God of whom we speak is the God of
Christian Revelation.   If this Revelation is true, then all that
we see of God's action can be accepted with confidence.   On the
other hand, if we consider Revelation to be meaningless, then
we must no longer ask the God of believers the reason for the
defeats of the Church of Christ, for which they profess He created
the world, nor the reason for the disproportions of the universe.
If we speak of God without recourse to the light of Revelation,
we are no longer speaking of the God of the Christians.   And any
other God would be very hard to accept.

The scars of sin

From the vantage point of the painful mystery of the Redemption,
let us cast a quick over-all glance at the history of life before the
coming of man.

A striking example of the useless expenditure of energy
is to be found in the many false starts life has made in the course
of evolution.   All along the road by which the various species

have progressed, we find blind-alleys where life lost its way. We have the testimony of many anatomical forms that appeared and disappeared without contributing in any way to progress. Countless mammoth and tiny animals have left nothing behind but their fossilized remains. As extinct branches of the genealogical tree of the living, they have not even been links opening the way to new developments. They are not intermediaries, but only waste products.

Moreover it is undeniable that in the living world today, no less than in the geological universe, there are swarms of superfluous beings. Besides the barren, uninhabitable lands on our planet, there are useless plants and animals, the parasites of creation.

In addition, there are the harmful animals, including the large fauna and micro-organisms which endanger the existence of living beings useful to man and even the existence of man himself. These are the pirates of life which science is trying with great effort to purge out of our world so that it may remain habitable for living beings endowed with spiritual life and inferior creatures useful to them.

The whole history of life is one of continual and ruthless warfare. As has been pointed out, the peace of the forests is made up of a perpetual carnage. All living things devour one another, and nature has shown great ingenuity in endowing the various animals with cruel weapons. Man is not innovating when he constantly uses his inventive faculties in the service of war. The forces that have fashioned the world of living beings have done so before him.

To explain the existence of living beings as the result of pure chance seems untenable. Whether we speak of an *élan vital* or use any other word to designate the dynamism that underlies the history of life, we cannot deny the presence of purposeful movement, of guided progression. And yet the groping march of life seems blind in so many cases, sometimes absurd and often cruel.

The biblical writers observed the disorder of the universe, and saw in it the prolongation of the disorder that has been in man since the Fall. Chapter II of Genesis shows the earth cursed as the result of sin, and Chapter I suggests the same thought in a more concrete way. In the world as originally planned by God, man is described as a vegetarian, and the animals were to eat only grass. The primordial universe was exempt from cruelty. According to God's primal intention, no living being was to shed blood. A corresponding view is to be found in Isaias. In messianic times, peace would return; there would be no more assaults against life; the lion would lie down with the lamb (cf. Is. 11: 6).

Obviously these symbolic words are not intended to be a course in natural history. But the idea that man perverted the universe in perverting himself offers us a criterion for interpreting our world. The world bears the marks of the wounds of sin, just as we do. In fact we must extend the idea of Genesis even further, as St. Paul does: the world, made for Christ, reflects the mystery of the Redemption; the sign of the crucifixion is engraved everywhere upon it.

When God set the universe in motion, He knew the risks He was incurring and accepted them. He squarely faced the possibility of sin and decided He would reach out, through the Incarnation and Redemption, to His creatures in their disgrace. He consented to the absurdity and cruelty into which men were to sink, and resolved to cure these evils by suffering them Himself in the person of His Son. He permitted that the universe, created in the service of man and meant to help him reach his goal, should go astray in the long course of its evolution amid absurdity and cruelty. He consented that the law of this earth should become the law that man would impose upon Christ when He came to deliver him from it: the law of suffering and failure.

It can be said that the evolution of life has the same characteristics as did Jesus' career on earth, since the Savior advanced toward the Resurrection amid trial and suffering. Likewise, the sorrowful face of the universe is the image of Christ's, and reminds us of the Paschal mystery, the mystery of death and resurrection which continues to unfold in the life of the Church.

The world was created with this mystery in mind, and a presage or vestige of this mystery is to be found everywhere.

We must hold fast to the conviction that in the beginning God made the whole world and everything in it good, as Genesis says emphatically and as the Fourth Lateran Council teaches. Correlatively, we must affirm that the initiator of evil in the world, Satan, is a creature totally dependent upon God. We must reject everything that can offend against Christian optimism, inspired by faith in the God of love, and everything that resembles Manichaean dualism. We must affirm simultaneously that God is love and that He is all-powerful.

It can be said that the world was marred by the sin of the angels, even before the sins of men. But to stop at sin does not give a complete picture. We understand sin only when we consider the mystery of mercy, when we meditate upon the work of the Redemption. That is why we relate all that is painful in the evolution of the world to the sufferings of Jesus. It is permissible, we think, to say that the universe may have been marked in advance with the sign of the cross, just as Mary was exempt from sin before the Redemption. To say in this context that God permitted the world to bear the features of the suffering Savior, long before the Passion and even before Adam's sin, does not contradict faith in primal love.

The supernatural and the vocations of men

Everything we have said concerning the destiny of the universe must be repeated with regard to the destiny of each one of us.

It is disappointing that our earth is so insignificant, so hostile to man, and that the Church is merely, in the words of the Gospel, a " little flock. " We would prefer our world to occupy a more central place in the universe; we would like man to be more completely the master, and the Church more powerful. God's love would then seem more believable, and faith more reasonable. Obviously, it would seem more natural, under the circumstances, to profess a Christian conception of the universe. But faith cannot be reduced to a profession of belief in a conception of the world. It does not consist merely in admitting an intellectually coordinated synthesis. It is first of all the humble trust of someone who places his life in the hands of another.

And just as we are very insignificant in the totality of creation, we are very small in our own eyes. A new source of disappointment! We would prefer to be proud of ourselves without reservation, to be freed from our errors of judgment, our pettiness, our inconstancy. It seems that it would be easier to believe in God's love if we had a sense of being worthy of it, if we felt we had some power of our own. We may not want to admit it, but a sort of inferiority complex prevents us from taking God's interest in us seriously. To be sure of Him, we would like to be sure of ourselves. Our inability to honestly think well of ourselves makes us reticent to trust God. In principle we affirm that God is good, but this is only an affirmation of principle. It is hard for us to live in practice as men who know in very truth that they are loved.

We feel the need of being satisfied with ourselves in order to be satisfied with God; of being successful in order to proclaim that He does great things; of being without serious sin in order to believe in His mercy. We need to think we are worth loving before we can believe that God loves us for no good reason, that is, simply because He is good. Such an attitude is evidently more naïve than the geocentrism of the Middle Ages. Now that the progress of the sciences has liberated us from the illusion that the earth is at the center of the universe, let us emancipate ourselves from a still greater form of childishness. Let us stop feeling the need to be centers of attraction that can draw God to themselves! Let us be humble enough to deem Him infinitely better than ourselves, and capable of loving us as we are.

We may object that if He really loved us He would heal our infirmities, or at least our moral ills. Obviously if we were in His place, we would act differently. We would begin by changing the data of universal gravitation, so as to give it a place more in keeping with the importance we attribute to it. Instead, let us allow God the liberty of leaving the earth where it is, just as Jesus dwelt upon it, and of leaving us with our limitations, since it has pleased Him to love us just as we are.

No, we have not yet finished drawing conclusions from astronomy that can be applied to our own personal behavior.

What God wants is to make us share His life. He wants to find us receptive, by the homage of our abandonment, to the divine work He desires to accomplish in human soil. Are we to say that nothing else interests Him?

God's primordial interest is the supernatural, and He can make it flourish munificently in poor natural soil. He can make a saint out of a man who is not very intelligent, out of a boor, or a neurotic. The Bible stresses God's independence of the artifacts of man. It is possible to grow rich, acquire culture, perfect one's talents, and yet remain a stranger to God, spiritually indigent. Conversely God can lavish His gifts on those who have never made a success of anything.

Are we to conclude that Christianity forces us to attribute value to human progress only in the measure that it is at the service of the supernatural?

Here again, if we are not to be misled, we must make distinctions. We must always distinguish between the thing " in itself " and the thing " as it concerns me. " And we must make this distinction first of all in the supernatural realm. In itself, prayer is more important than work. But, insofar as it concerns me, God's call may require me not to devote myself to a purely contemplative life. What God wants in the concrete is that each one should answer his own personal vocation. It would be an error to enter the religious life in order to live the most perfect life possible. One must enter it only if one is called; it is not God's good pleasure that we rush into it on our own initiative, without waiting for His invitation. The only way to clearly see the course we must follow as Christians is through union with God. Solitary reflection on our part will inevitably lead to mistakes.

To speak concretely, there are men whom God draws to Himself not by the path of faith, but simply by the path of good will. No theologian will maintain that unbelievers, ignorant of the Church's existence or separated from her by invincible psychological obstacles, are rejected by the God of love. If they have no religion, then the only purpose they can give their life is the attainment of authentic human progress. That is their own way of seeking God, and in the concrete that is what He expects of them. On the part of the believers whom He calls to work in the world, God expects an effort comparable to that of the unbelievers, but quickened by the theological life. For a Christian to renounce life in the world for the cloister, for example, might in certain instances merely be a flight from responsibility. In practice, each one must strive, his soul strengthened by prayer and attentive to circumstances, to fashion the Christian success

God seeks to achieve within him, and which will never be exactly like any other.

But even though the most perfect in itself is not necessarily so for me, nothing can be sanely desirable for me unless it has value in itself. It must at least have the lowly value of being useful, of being attainable. There would be no Christian vocation to work if work did not have a universal value, independently of its own providential sanctifying value. Everything authentically human to which God calls both believers and unbelievers according to their own particular path, has value in His eyes. Indeed things, of their nature estimable and desirable, can be used in the service of evil, or be sought with an intention that, concretely, is contrary to God's intention. God's work can be used against Him, when one is not attentive to His call.

If God allowed Christ's blood to be shed, it was not because He had no interest in this blood. If God tolerates that the Church be limited in her personnel, it is not because He has no interest in pagans and infidels. If God has made saints of uneducated men, it is not because He has no interest in culture. These are "wastes" only in our eyes. But we are obviously unable to penetrate God's thoughts. If God were not mysterious and baffling, He would not be God. He would be merely a personification of our ideas, built to our measurements.

He knows what He is doing, but He thinks with His heart. And that disconcerts our businessmen's calculations.

Just Because we see it this way

The completion of history

To understand the history of the world in Christian terms, we must evidently focus our attention on something beyond this history. We must consider its completion. The evolution of the universe and the evolution of the Church will reveal their secret only at the end of time.

What is first in the order of intention is last in the order of execution. God's first purpose, around which everything else revolves, is the eternal fulfillment He is preparing during the course of time. To understand the meaning of creation, we must think of the "new creation."

In his Apocalypse St. John calls to mind the renewal of all things, for which all things were created. He describes the realizations toward which God has been guiding His creatures from the beginning of time, such as the new Jerusalem and the triumph of the Lamb.

The Apocalypse, the final portion of the Bible, explains Genesis which opens Revelation. In disposing the world with the solicitude described in the accounts of creation, God had ultimate unity in mind. In setting the universe in motion, He had in view the ultimate gathering together which had its beginning here on earth in the Church. The whole history of the world is a preparation for this completion.

The history of the visible universe unfolds between two decisive events: the irrevocable choice made by the angels, and the eternal encounter between humanity and God. The spiritual world encompasses the material world, and also man who decides his own destiny and that of the universe by accepting God or rejecting Him. The rupture among the angels had repercussions among men. Adam's sin is the echo of the Satanic revolt. Man is a battleground for other forces than his own. He is motivated by inspirations from the invisible world, and he in turn draws the material world along with him.

After these confrontations, we shall decipher the meaning of the entire universe, as well as its true dimensions. We shall see the scope and depth of the reciprocal influences between the visible and the invisible.

The eternal kingdom of Christ should not be pictured as a place where those who are with God differ among themselves only by their degree of sanctity and are distinguished only by their rank. Heaven is the completion of personality. Men of the East will be recognizable from men of the West, men of the stagecoach era from those of the atomic age. They will not have the same spiritual physiognomy. The places where we live also take up their abode within us. The things we fashion, shape us. The civilization to which we belong leaves its imprint on our life of faith. Everything that concerns us puts its mark upon us, and for eternity.

It is this completion of man, and within him of the world where he lives, that God is pursuing. Everything He does contributes to the formation of the ultimate physiognomy of His work.

The Incarnation and the Redemption are prolonged in us. We shall fully understand their meaning only when they have attained their plenitude. When all things have been gathered up in Christ, we shall no longer need to believe. We shall understand that everything has been made for Him.

The prolongation of the Incarnation and Redemption is the Church. The world was created for the Church of heaven, where all those who have belonged visibly or invisibly to the Church of earth will meet. It is only in this final realization that we shall perceive the true dimensions of what, to all outward appearances, is only a " little flock " here on earth.

The world was made for man, but ultimately for risen man. The consummation of the divine work will manifest what man has done with the world entrusted to him and what man has become through this world. It will also show what God has done with the world and with man, namely, everything that He expected of them from the beginning of time.

When the invisible has been made visible, then the true face of the visible will be revealed. When we see the face of God...

PART TWO

FAITH IN GOD THE SAVIOR

III   Is christianity a humanism?

Saving man...

There is much talk about " saving man. " What do we mean when we speak of it in the name of our Christian faith? What does Jesus offer man when He comes to him as his " Savior "?

To our way of thinking as believers, it is sin and its consequences from which man must be saved. Sin, that many-faced evil, is not merely a disgrace, it is slavery. It is not simply a degradation of man himself, it is coming under the power of Satan.

To be saved is not primarily to be emancipated from the limitations imposed upon us by our nature, our heredity, our past, and the milieu in which we live; it is to be no longer cut off from God, it is to be His friend. Sanctifying grace is a divine presence within us, whereas the state of sin is an isolation. In this isolation we are not merely left to our own devices, we become serfs of hell.

Solitude and communion

The human condition is a fabric of relationships. To be saved is to be in communion with God. Damnation is the shattering of this union and becoming entangled in other bonds—bonds which fetter us to the devil. To understand Christian salvation we must look beyond the being to be saved, i.e., beyond what man is, and see the One toward whom he is going. We must consider concretely the One who dwells in him and moves him, the One in whom he trusts and founds his life. What invisible presence haunts him, what exchange nourishes his soul? Is he with God? Or on the contrary is he alone, that is to say, with Satan, whose tyranny isolates? The infernal world is a world of isolated beings.

To be saved is to break away from Satan's dominion and to cleave to Jesus. It is to enter into the "admirable exchange" of the Incarnation, to cease to offer resistance to the divine magnet, and to be open to its action. It is to be so authentically with Jesus as to become like Him, to be so truly like Him as to be sons of the Father in Him. To be saved is to participate in the meeting of the divine and the human accomplished by the Incarnation of the Word, and this Incarnation will attain its fullest dimensions only in the Resurrection, the general Resurrection.

Another Christ

The salvation God offers us in the Person of His incarnate Son is something quite different from a change in the conditions of our life, and quite different also from progress solely in terms of ourselves. It is passage from a solitude imposed by Satan to a communion given by God. Human procedures may encourage man to be more fully "human," but God alone can offer him the prospect of being with God, which is a superhuman way of being human.

On every page of the Bible man is offered a choice: to want a salvation that will make him autonomous, or to seek his salvation in life with God. For centuries the salvation pictured in the Sacred Books by images in abundance was thought to be merely temporal and earthly. And yet these images were but commentaries on the oft-repeated promise: "You shall belong to Me," "You shall walk before My face," "You shall be My people and I shall be your God." In Revelation, salvation is always fundamentally a belonging to God, a life with Him which the Incarnation was to demonstrate as being a life truly in Him.

The object of our hope is not primarily increased well-being, but Someone. Similarly, a young engaged couple look forward not to a life of greater comfort, or even to the fulfillment of their personalities, but to a life together. Every man who reflects on what he is going to do with his life has a choice between two courses. Either he can perfect himself in rigorous solitude, by developing his talents, by submitting to methods of physical and moral improvement; or else he can become a different man by being receptive to sympathy and love, and accepting the dependence inherent in friendship and marriage. Now Christianity offers us the second type of fulfillment. It is not a salvation to be achieved through a technique, but a transformation produced by contact with God. But, as we shall emphasize, this second form of salvation does not destroy the values sought by the first. Rather, it places strictly human salvation in second place where it belongs. At the outset it eliminates pride, which vitiates life in the measure that it excludes dependence on God.

God interrogates the men of our era just as He has interrogated the men of every era. He demands a choice between two ideals: the ideal of solitude and the ideal of filial dependence which will be consummated in eternal friendship.

Independence is in very truth a snare. The condition of hell is not autonomy but slavery. Here on earth, to found one's life on pride is to choose not liberty but its caricature. There are human associations that shut us up within ourselves, influences that are like prisons. Satan's action on the world is of this nature. It cuts man off from God, inciting him to pride, the root of all sin. Man can reject God with full knowledge and consent. That is the sin against the Spirit which makes it impossible for God to save man, since salvation must be freely accepted and not accomplished by compulsion. Man can also reject God and rally to Satan through ignorance, without understanding of the terrible import of his choice. That is most often the case of the unbeliever. In this situation, God can still have the last word, and God's last word is always one of mercy.

Total communion on earth and in the world beyond

In the strict sense, Christian salvation belongs to the world beyond. It is being with God, seeing Him face to face, with no danger that the encounter will ever end. And true life, true light, consists in living together with Him—not merely by His side—without reticence and without danger of inconstancy on our part.   The universe of isolation that is hell is the kingdom of real death and darkness.

The salvation that is close friendship with the living God consists not only of His gifts but also of God Himself.   The life and light that Scripture speaks of are the privileges of the Most High; and it is this life and light that we share.   He does not merely lavish external favors upon us, He gives us Himself.   His presence irradiates His creatures, and the union between man and the Transcendent becomes so close that God's life becomes his very own.

By the same token, salvation is unity among men.   Not a coexistence or an entente cordiale, but a cracking open, through contact with God, of the carapace that imprisons men and makes them strangers to one another.   Even here on earth, certain personalities are so outgoing that they create a climate of contagious sympathy around them.   Their mere presence dispels dissensions before they can find expression, as well as tacit distrusts and aggressive attitudes that divide souls without their knowing.   Here on earth, the deep-seated unity of a group is less the fruit of superficial dispositions of good will than the rallying of all to a common human value, or better still to a person for whom they feel deep attraction.   Thus the encounter with God—Father, Son, and Spirit—accomplished in a total surrender that will make us truly members of His family, will bring us close to one another as no human rallying can.   Together with God Himself, and with His divine life, a supernaturally fraternal life will also be given us.

Here on earth we hope for our personal salvation and for the salvation of the world.   These are two aspects of one and the same reality.   For in heaven we shall belong to God and be together in fraternal unity.   We shall have been won at once for God and for His kingdom; we shall be new men and a new city. A new way of being ourselves—by being of God and in God—will be a new way of belonging to others.

The invisible communion of earth: the life of grace

Our salvation, which consists in complete communion with God, begins here on earth. Already in this world we are no longer alone. The meeting between men and their Savior who gathers them into Himself is a reality here and now. But this presence of the eternal in time is primarily a hidden reality. What is most fundamental about Christian salvation is hidden from all eyes except those of faith.

Reality in the deepest sense is beyond human perception. Here on earth the reality that surpasses all others is grace: present in the child who is not yet conscious, in the dying man who has lost consciousness, and in the abnormal human being who will never be conscious of the world around him. In these beings there is little of the human, and yet so much of the divine.

Life with God here on earth is first of all this mysterious symbiosis. The salvation that matters most is this meeting of heaven and earth, beyond the realm of perceptible reality. A child may be medically doomed to an early death or be unable to grow in the normal life of the spirit. He may not live until he attains the age of reason, or perphaps never attain psychological adulthood. He is lost to humanism and to the social relations of earth, but not to his eternal destiny as a man. His Savior is with him because of his baptism, and the seed of the kingdom has been planted in his soul.

When God takes complete possession of man, man will be truly himself in all his constituent faculties. In heaven there will no longer be any crippled, or diseased, or ignorant, or discouraged men. When man is completely united to God he will be what God has always wanted him to be. By contrast, man as we know him now has become a caricature of what God expects of him. Humanity in all its perfection is represented only in Christ and in His Mother, for they alone were associated with the divine life in soul and body. No other human creature possesses the fullness of human perfection, for everyone else has been disfigured by the devil's evil works. It was even so for Christ during His mortal life. He made Himself like sinners in consenting to suffer and die.

Conscious communion here on earth: the theological life

The world in which we live is one that has been ravished from
God and yet is already reconquered by Him. Divine friendship
dwells within it and restores it to health at a depth not revealed
by human behavior. Original sin has been remitted, and thus
the continuity between earth and heaven has been restored. But
the presence in the world of the Father's love results in an upsurge
of love toward Him. Imprisoned in their human infirmities for
part or all of their earthly lives, men still strive to attain the
theological life wherever the path of consciousness remains open.
The faith that God expects of us is the loyalty of creatures bearing
the stigmata of sin; it is a faith that acknowledges the damage
wrought upon the whole human race by Adam's fall, and therefore
it is a means of emerging from this disgrace. The theological
life is a victory over sin and its consequences, a victory of a different order than the healing of the mind or the elimination of
disease by means of psychological re-education or medical cures.
The faith that is perpetuated in hope and charity has the power to
save because it is a cleaving to Christ, a surrender to God. It
consists in accepting God's plan to make us His children
despite our unworthiness. Its normal extension is the amending
of man's moral life, but it is not limited to moral progress
alone.

The Christian's effort to live a virtuous life is a translation
of the divine message into the language of faith. It is a form of
the life of prayer. This effort may be paralyzed by temperament,
heredity, habits, and environment, and in great part fail to attain
its goal. Faith demands calm acceptance of the failures that
cannot be avoided. It demands renouncement of ambition, even
for spiritual successes in which human pride may be a motivating
force. It demands an effort toward conversion because the Master
requires and deserves it, and not for our own satisfaction. Faith
asks us to free ourselves from our human concern about success,
and go to God with the same eagerness whether or not we can
see tangible results of our efforts.

Thus faith leads to something essentially different from
a humanistic equilibrium. In borderline cases, if a man's theolo-

gical life is weak and his temperament vicious, he may relapse after his conversion into the same sins as often as before he found God. He may already have been struggling stoically against his evil tendencies, and continue to fight without any noticeable improvement. But in the measure that his faith gains strength, a change occurs in the spirit that motivates him and also in his attitude toward the results of his efforts. Formerly he fought for himself and with his own resources; he had to face his failures as well as his successes alone. Now the motive that impels him is his trust in God's merciful love. He is sustained by the same faith in love in the face of defeat as well as victory.

Faith is absolutely incompatible with the spirit that leads to sin, namely, the will to self-sufficiency. It implies a renewal of moral life that is the authentic expression of a vigorous loyalty to the Master. But while faith eliminates the sin of malice, it may have little power against human weaknesses born of temperament or habit. In fact it may remedy such failings only gradually and after many disappointments. The essential changes that faith brings about lie in the climate of moral behavior, but in some cases faith will be less effective than medical care in obtaining results.

Evidently the imperfections into which a man may fall despite a strong and active faith will rarely if ever be sins. We must therefore declare that on the level of true morality faith is always profoundly transforming. However, since it does not have a directly curative effect on a perverse temperament or on a poorly enlightened intellect, it may at times have a rather limited effect, despite rightness of intention, on actions that are objectively to be condemned. The point we are trying to make here is that Christian conversion is of an entirely different order than the improvement of one's mode of behavior according to exterior criteria. It is of a higher order than the reformations produced by rigorous effort, by adherence to an ideal of purity, or by medical means.

The salvation begun here on earth, therefore, is not primarily a way of escaping the many failings that weigh us down, but essentially a liberation from the self-satisfaction or despair that incite us to try to get along without God. What is important is not that the vicious man cease to be vicious, but that, in his efforts and in his defeats, he no longer be alone, that he cry out to God, acknowledging his indigence and his trust.

The salvation begun on earth is union with God. It is of a different nature from the human battle for morality, and different in nature from the human healing of the psyche. Salvation is supernatural. It is communion with God in a theological life that inspires every moral effort. It is something that man cannot acquire for himself either by a humanistic ideal or by a technique of psychotherapy. He can only receive it and want it in union with God who offers it to him.

The Christian attitude finds its deepest expression in the supernatural about-face which makes man think of God rather than of himself, strive to live in union with God rather than desire to be more noble as a man. This is the most precious part of the Church's heritage. Her essential task is to perpetuate the flame of faith here on earth, rather than build a " Christian civilization. " The most important cause she has to promote is not what she may have in common with a philosophically inspired humanism, but something she alone can offer: the invitation to accept the supernatural salvation that God wants to accomplish within us, even on this earth, if we will only give our *fiat*.

To understand the true value of the Christian Church, in contrast to a mutual aid society for self-mastery, we must keep her supernatural invitation in mind. The Church must not be placed on the same footing with an organization for moral progress. Religion cannot be reduced to a way of improving man's human attitudes. The essential religious problem is not to make man more human, but to make him surrender himself to God who will save him, providing he sincerely wants to be saved.

The theological life and the demands of the moral life

Earthly ideals and human techniques can facilitate conversion to Christ through faith. Vice can render a man insensible to the divine call, just as a man's environment can make it impossible for him to know Christ. Human obstacles may make faith impossible. For example, the absence of the Church in mission lands makes Christ unknowable to many. Likewise, lack of psychological preparation may render man incapable of understanding His call. The solitude of a man who rejects God may not be a culpable solitude, and he may be enslaved without any deliberation or consent on his part. In such a case, obviously, Satan has won only a pseudo-victory. Pagans in good faith are not rejected by God. But the Church has no right to resign herself even to this transitory victory by the enemy. To make faith conquer, she must use all the weapons at her command: morality, intellectual training, good living conditions, as well as progress in the psychological and pedagogical sciences.

Nor can the Church resignedly watch man's encounter with God fail to lead to a liberation from vice. While this may not be the primal aspect of her mission, it is not a matter of option for the believer or for those who guide him. This moral purification is the normal expression of loyalty to God, which, as we have said, implies an authentic conversion.

Beyond all systems of morality and among all religions, Christianity has this unique feature: it involves the personal surrender of man to his personal God—in a spirit of trust and not of fear—so that God may accomplish a truly divine work in man. In this light all sin is to be deplored, especially because it is proof of an imperfect surrender to God, consciously and willfully imperfect in varying degrees. Sin is to be deplored also because it makes more difficult the abandonment to divine mercy demanded by the theological life of faith, hope, and love.

This evil consequence of sin needs to be stressed. When a man feels he is his own master and untouched by disgrace, he is in danger of no longer feeling the need for God and for the Redemption. But after he has experienced his weakness, he is in danger of not daring to believe in the fidelity of God's love. Awareness of the apparent futility of effort threatens the theological life itself. It is hard to persevere when we cannot take courage from our own victories, but must count solely on God's benevolence. It is hard to go to God apparently empty-handed, to determine on the austere self-stripping that awareness of persistent weakness demands. It is not easy to admit that in the eyes of God, it is our effort to achieve filial union that counts far more than the results of this effort. It is hard to consent to be a child of few talents whom the Father loves just as he is, without any need to bolster His affection by seeing him act like a talented child. It is heroic to live such a life of faith joyfully, and yet this is demanded of all of us in varying degrees. For our successes will always be mingled with defeats, and we shall always remain indigent in one way or another.

This steadfastness in our theological dispositions, despite repeated failures, is not merely difficult for human strength, it is strictly impossible. The theological life can spring up and persevere in us only through grace, a many-sided grace that we must accept from the depths of our soul, with everything we are, loyal to the Redeemer who will draw all our faculties to Himself. It is a grace that we must accept with ever-renewed loyalty and notwithstanding our repeated falls.

Irrespective of these bonds with the theological life which are of concern only to Christians, breaches of the natural law are to be deplored by both believer and unbeliever fot the same reason: they represent failure at the human level. God is the author of natural law, and the Law of Revelation does not abolish it.

The theological life and the " sense of sin "

We have spoken of the way sin endangers the theological life. In order to have a better understanding of the psychological renewal accomplished by faith, hope, and charity, let us consider how the believer should look upon his weakness before God. The " Christian sense of sin " is very different from the instinctive anxiety experienced after a taboo is violated, and also from the sense of disgrace that often follows a fall from chastity, for example, that the modern psychological disciplines have analyzed at length.

Obviously the sense of sin is not to be confused with anxiety or depression rooted outside the limits of clear-headed reason. Nor is it to be identified with admission of breaking a law. Awareness of being a sinner is very different from the sense of unworthiness we may have if we have repudiated principles we have professed or broken the rules of honor. Nor is it to be reduced to a sense of responsibility. All these can exist in a solitary soul, whereas the sense of sin is an awareness of the gravity of an offense directed essentially against Someone, against the God of love. The sense of sin is awareness of the disorder implicit in disloyalty to God's love, an awareness illumined by faith in the Father's love. We have a " sense of sin " only in the measure that we have a " sense of God." We can admit we are sinners in the Christian sense only if we believe in grace. We do not really know what sin is unless we think of it in terms of forgiveness.

The sentiment of being a sinner is a sentiment of guilt, but a guilt from which instinctive anguish, as well as rancor against self and against others, have been exorcised. It is free of despair and aggressiveness. It is sorrow in the presence of the merciful love of the One we have rejected, rather than sadness born of mulling over our own misery. Faith in God's love must exorcise our sense of success, our smug complacency, no less than our feeling of defeat and the resulting discontent.

Our awareness of having sinned is made keener and healthier when we place ourselves in God's presence. It ceases to be harmful when solitude ends. While it becomes more acute, it no longer paralyzes us but acts as a stimulus. Whereas it is sterile to look within ourselves with remorse, it is very fruitful to place ourselves in God's presence in a spirit of repentance. In the first case there is isolation; in the second, communion. Repentance is rooted in love. What annihilates us and gives psychiatrists their practice is the habit of holding unending private conversations with ourselves. By contrast, repentance gives new impetus to our efforts.

That is why the saints, who are anything but despondent, never tire of calling themselves sinners. They admit they are poor sinners, but they do so in a spirit of trust, peace, and even joy. When they confess their sins, they are thinking not of themselves but of God. They do not drone out their own sad story, but sing of God's mercy. They do not curse themselves, but magnify Him. In truth, the sense of sin is less a way of knowing ourselves than of knowing God. It consists in the knowledge of two things that mutually clarify each other: knowledge of ourselves in the light of our faith in the Redemption;

knowledge of the love of God as contrasted with the unworthiness of its object.

Whence a paradox: for the Christian sin is the supreme evil, the only real disgrace; and yet for the Christian sin has little importance, for what really matters is the merciful love of the Most High. Does not St. Augustine proclaim that for those who love God all things end well, even their sins? And St. Thérèse of the Child Jesus affirmed in the last sentence of her *Autobiography*, written in pencil as she lay on her sickbed, that even if she had committed all the sins that can be committed she would go to God with the same trust and love.

What is it that matters enormously, and yet does not matter? First of all, it is our past sins. We must live as forgiven sinners. We profess a religion of Redemption. Therefore we cannot go to God with proudly raised heads, as if His crucified Son were not between Him and us. Because we believe in a love so far above all human love that it impelled the Father to give us His only-begotten Son, we cannot be stopped by fear of divine resentment. We must go to God with a love born of His forgiveness.

Secondly, our future sins are vastly important, and yet do not matter. We must do the impossible to avoid them, and yet calmly accept the fact of our weakness without yielding to anxiety when we think of the relapses into sin that will probably halt our progress. What God expects of us is not the sort of effort that pagans are capable of, but the confident energy of sons assured of their Father's love. And the effort born of this certitude will be proportionate to the vigor of our theological life. When divine grace informs all our actions, what would have been impossible to mere human strength often becomes possible and easy. And what we have said of the theological life itself applies as well to all moral effort quickened by this life.

The example of the Christian attitude in the face of defeat, and of the incomparably serious defeat that is mortal sin, clearly reveals the kind of spiritual vitality, the theological life of faith, hope, and charity brings to our souls. It is not the human fulfillment to be found in a psychic cure or in the pleasures of a cultivated mind. No, it is the liberation that comes from surrender to God. Increased well-being may be either the condition or the result of this surrender. The Christian who seeks

God will still want psychological balance and culture, but for him these things will be transfigured by a supernatural light. Instead of wanting to act alone, the believer will tend to do all things " together " with his God.

This spiritual transformation can be compared to those that result from purely human forms of communion, such as marriage, friendship, mutual trust, and comradeship. The theological life is very much like human ways of breaking out of solitude, but it differs profoundly from them just as God differs from man. When communion with the transcendent God is at the origin of a spiritual transformation, the resulting oneness and release from tension go infinitely deeper than is possible in any earthly exchange. There is no denying, of course, that our faith is often weak. And yet it restores every fiber of our being in proportion to its vigor and intensity.

The theological life and the demands of human progress

The religious effort of a man who wants to be more perfectly a man must necessarily join forces with his moral effort. Morality has its own value, independent of the spirit of faith that informs it in the believer's soul. The Church has condemned the idea that the acts of an unbeliever are necessarily displeasing to God. The progress of morality, therefore, has a twofold interest for the believer: first, because it is bound up with the normal progress of the theological life; and secondly, because it has value in itself that no man can ignore.

The fundamental psychological transformation implicit in the salvation begun here on earth consists in receiving God in a spirit of faith, in learning to know the Master whose sons we agree to become. As we have already stressed at length, this is the mark of grace upon the world at the level of the humanly perceptible. This is what makes our universe different from what it would have been if the way had not been prepared for Christ's coming to earth and if He had not actually come. It is something no earthly humanism can offer, and it is the most fundamental transformation in human behavior wrought by the Christian religion. But this life of faith is necessarily integrated

in a striving for moral perfection. And moral effort has a human
value of its own. To disregard this fact is a form of clericalism,
that is not always avoided. [1]

Besides, the progress of morality is not the only human
interest of the believer. What we have just said applies as well
to everything that has authentic human value and can make union
with God easier or more complete. This would include improvement in living conditions, as well as in psychical and physical
health. While religion is something altogether different from
any form of humanism, it forbids us to deliberately reject any
form of humanism. God is not indifferent to man in any sphere
of human activity. [2]

The role of religion with regard to efforts to create "a more human world"

The first question we must ask ourselves, in the face of Christian
Revelation and humanisms that leave out God, is not whether
religion is a factor making for peace among individuals and
peoples, for a more moral life, for better psychological balance.
The first question is not whether the supernatural work of God
does or does not serve the natural progress of man. Obviously the
essential question is whether God exists and calls us, whether
the Church is telling us the truth. Now this does not exclude
another problem, regarding the services religion renders to man
and in what respect " Christian civilization " is a human heritage
to which no man can remain indifferent. We have the right
to make the most effective use of what the Church has
accomplished to perfect the human side of man. And yet we
must not forget that this human effort is carried on as part of
the religious effort to which the Church rightly gives primacy.

---

[1] The Thomistic line of thought tends to recognize a value in profane
realities in themselves. In consequence, it attributes a certain autonomy to
them (independence of the State in its order, etc.). The Augustinian line of
thought, on the contrary, tends to integrate the profane into the religious.

[2] We shall not consider here the arguments between the proponents of
" incarnation " and the partisans of " transcendence. " What we have to say
here will be admitted by both groups, but with varying overtones. The differences will relate in particular to the ways of conceiving the gratuitousness of
the supernatural and the corruption of nature by sin.

The essential effort of the believer is not to attain self-mastery, to become better balanced, or to be more generous and useful to his neighbor. Religion is not first of all a way of being more perfectly man. It is above all a surrender to God. The essential effort is the one demanded by the life of faith. It is more fundamental to be a believer than to be moral, well-balanced, and self-sacrificing. This does not mean—need we stress again?—that moral health, psychological maturity, and unselfishness are merely accessory. A man can remain vicious and yet turn to God in his misery; he can be psychologically degenerate and yet accept his degradation with trust in the Lord. And conversely a man can overcome a vice and still not be reconciled with God. But no man can put his faith in Christ and claim that obedience to His commandments is unimportant, particularly those that concern his attitude toward his neighbor.

We cannot deny that often we aspire only to become—or to help others to become—more fully developed human beings, more moral, psychologically better balanced. We make use of the attitudes of faith as means to promote a humanistic ideal. We seek in religion a technique analogous to the methods of improving the human race found in many works on self-mastery and influencing others. Or perhaps we turn to religion because it offers a way to a more dignified life, to social progress. Evidently we must do these things, for we must not deprive ourselves of the help of God in our efforts to achieve the progress that God Himself desires. But we must not confuse the end with the means.

We must remember that even if the social and medical sciences, psychological techniques and humanistic ideals had achieved complete success, religion would still not have lost its reason for being. There is much talk about making a " more human world. " We must realize that even if such an undertaking had attained its goal, it still could not claim to take the place of religion.

The Christian religion belongs to another order than secular humanisms. There is a vast difference between merely making man more human and surrendering him into God's hands; between enabling him to possess the world more perfectly and eading him to Christ; between perfecting him through his own resources and giving him access to communion with God. Nevertheless, while Christian faith has primarily other goals in view, it also has the obligation to take an interest in everything that elevates man.

In the preceding pages we have laid particular stress on what is unique about the authentic religious attitude, and on the danger of confusing divine friendship with ideals conceived by men. In concluding we would like to stress the complementary aspect of the view we have expressed. We have said that the progress of all that is human should be of interest to the believer. But we must go further and emphasize that placing man in communion with God is an indirect, but unrivaled way of making him more perfectly a man.

There is need, of course, of taking into account the diversity of ways that lead to God. Some are called by God to withdraw from the world. Others, on the contrary, are sent out into the world, where, thanks to their faith, they will engage in earthly tasks with a purity of intention that will make their efforts incomparably fruitful. Let us think of all the great works Christian charity has inspired. Let us remember what faith commands in the way of respect for the human person, as a being created by a God of love and redeemed by Jesus Christ. We could also point out how loyalty to the personal God and to the God-made-man lead to a concrete attitude of esteem and mutual aid that is very different from adherence to principles inspired by abstract theories on the destiny of humanity.

Search for the absolute requires a detachment from the finite that transfigures our way of looking at earthly realities. It does not make us strangers to this world, but it results in our being present in it in a way that is more profoundly human as well as supernatural.

Regardless of earthly progress, man will always remain the victim of suffering and death. The theological life changes the meaning of these trials. It makes man emerge from them, and in a way that is not to be compared with escapism or a stoical callousness to pain.

The Christian life safeguards man against earthly happiness, even as it strengthens him in suffering. It prevents transitory pleasures from imprisoning him in an easy life devoid of perspective, and gives him access, even here on earth, to a peace and joy that he can never know if he remains isolated from God.

These thoughts should be developed as applying not only to individual cases, but to the whole Church and to her entire history. True, a glance at the Christian community and at its past reveals many blemishes. But we can be proud of the civilizing work the Church has done through the centuries and is still doing today in countries like our own, as well as in mission lands and among disinherited peoples.

There are many imperfections within the Church, and many authentic values outside the Church. To judge them, we must first interpret them. And to interpret them correctly, we cannot be satisfied with tabulating facts and figures. We must also understand their underlying spirit. The Christian ideal of humanism must be seen once more in the context of the spirit of the theological virtues, if we want to understand the mainspring of an effort which, despite its deficiencies, possesses a rare human quality as well as unique religious value.

The heart of the message of Revelation is not a conception of man, but a conception of God. It is from this treasure that all the other doctrinal views of the Church flow, just as in our Christian life all interest in human matters springs from our belief in God.

Having an open mind and heart

When we say that the primordial work of the Church is the supernatural communion of man with God, and the communion of men among themselves in God, when we say that this truly divine work has become incarnate in the progress of civilizations without becoming identified with them, we are saying that the Church can and must be attentive to every form of humanism without being the prisoner of any one of them.

Even in our religious life as Christians, we have something to learn from India and Islam. The One who teaches us in the Church also speaks to us about His plan for the world in the person of every man and woman. Since every human being is a divine image, the living God manifests Himself in each one in some way. If we go out to the pagans with the poverty of spirit called for by the Gospel, God will enrich us through them. The history of the Church, of theology, and of sanctity are made up not only of gifts but also of exchanges.

Clearly, there can be no question here of allowing ourselves to be seduced by a religious syncretism in which enslavement to our own convenience would take the place of fidelity to God. The question here is simply one of understanding what the God of our faith asks of us.

It is in this same spirit that we must open our minds and hearts to everything that, in any way whatever, is different from our way of being a man, and of making man more human.

IV The Church, a mystery of salvation

Truth...

In asking ourselves what God expects of us in His work of salvation, we must approach the question not in terms of our own ability but from the vantage point of truth. Certainly we want our action to be efficacious, but above all we want it to conform to the truth.

The great realities: life and unity

The fundamental realities are invisible. It might be helpful to remember that we are so surrounded by visible realities that we are in danger of losing our sense of mystery, so essential to all Christian thought.

Let us start out with an example. A family is not an economic association, the father of a family is something more than the foreman in a factory. In what respect? In the business world, we place property or labor in common—in a human way, of course, and therefore implying a certain self-giving—in order to attain a material goal. What constitutes a family, on the other hand, is the gift of the persons involved in view of accomplishing a work of love. And that is why marriage is the only contract in this world that is indissoluble. The family is an image of the Church. There is a mystery of the family— and the underlying reality of the family is much deeper than the joint accomplishment of an exterior work—just as there is a mystery of the Church. And the indissolubility of marriage reminds us of the eternal validity of the baptismal character.

The deepest realities are invisible, and the deepest human problems are problems of unity. We are vaguely aware of it. The important questions of our life are these: the question of our own interior cohesion, of our encounter with our fellows on the level of familial, social, national, or international relations, and above all the question of our encounter with God. The answers to these problems that haunt us are to be found in the great mysteries of our faith, which are mysteries of unity. The God of Christian Revelation has manifested Himself to us as a God with a passion for unity.

The God who has spoken to us through the Lord Jesus is not merely the First Cause of the philosophers, or the primordial Intellect that orders the universe. He is more than a principle upon which the social order is founded. He is all these things, and above and beyond that He is Someone. And not only is He Someone; He is an exchange between Persons, a Dialogue, a Communion. He is the Father, Son, and Holy Spirit, in full reciprocity, the mutual gift between them being total, so total that each of the Divine Persons is purely and simply the gift of Himself. The Father is not someone who is a father, but Fatherhood that is Someone. The divine life that we know through faith is the ultimate triumph of the person, i. e., being oneself in communion with another. We believe not merely in ideas but in a personal God, in a God who is love. We believe in the Father and the Son, in the welling up of their mutual love which is the Holy Spirit. And we believe this divine life has been given to our world. Our faith makes us welcome the grace that is a presence within the created world of the life and unity that are in God.

Life and unity are inseparable. To live is to live with. While this is true even of biological life, it is true in a far deeper sense of the life of the spirit. For every spiritual being, to live is to live together. This is something we observe every day. We diminish ourselves when we close ourselves to others, when we yield to the temptation to isolate ourselves out of sullenness, rancor, or discouragement. We are less ourselves when we become indifferent to those around us. When we break off the dialogue, when we wall ourselves up in silence, out of hostility or despair, we are committing an assault on life. Our daily experience gives

Hast thou
heard a word
against
thy neighbor?
Let it die
within thee.

Ecclus. 19:10

within ourselves is Satanic,
becomes the condition of
ly, we live again when we
ding. We would truly be
constrained fraternal com-
be ourselves in this com-

nd God called the world into
life and unity. He invented
with him. Time after time
nostalgia and repeats this
that speak of a mutual love
people, and I shall be your
ore of us than service. He
d so that we might love Him.
call to man in these words:
d with thy whole heart, with
rength." Jesus clarified the
ours as well, in these terms:
ants, but My friends." The
Christian life and apostolate to which we are called are above all a
friendship, a friensdhip with God and with men. God's work in
this world springs from His heart, and it finds expression in us
through love.

God is not content to offer us gifts. He gives us Himself.
He does not merely ask gifts of us, He asks us to give ourselves
to Him. The total gift of self which is love is never possible
except in a person-to-person relationship, in a dialogue. The
total gift that God asks of us is impossible for man left to his own
resources. It is possible only when man, actively passive, accepts
the dialogue that God awakens in him, opens his soul to grace,
and offers up to God faith, hope, and charity.

Life and unity in the mystery of the Redemption

It is here that we touch upon the heart of the mystery of the
Redemption and of the Church. The mystery of the Blessed
Trinity is prolonged in another mystery of unity, the mystery

of God-made-man through the Incarnation, and in the mystery of unity that is also the mystery of the Mystical Body. We who believe in the unity of the Trinitarian life, also believe in the unity of the Godhead and human nature in the Person of the Word Incarnate. And finally we believe in the vocation of all men to unity in the Lord Jesus.

God's call to live together with Him is manifested with explosive power in the Incarnation of the Son, in the life and death among men of the Second Person of the Blessed Trinity, and in His resurrection in us. The eternal Son has been given to us. Not only has He assumed our nature, but He has become a member of our sinful race. The Virgin Mary is at once the daughter of the rebels and the Mother of the God of holiness. He has lived in our state of disgrace, like us in all things except sin. And He lived this life of fallen man until He died the death of the cross to which men had nailed Him. And in so doing, He made man's condition something altogether new. He transformed it into a resurrection mysteriously begun here on earth by the life of grace, and that will be consummated in heaven. As a living and efficacious call to unity, Jesus came to make us, in Him, true children of the Father and truly brothers.

The entire Gospel is an invitation to the authentic life of communion. God did not limit Himself to being our sinful world's benefactor while remaining outside it. He has given us His Son to live among us, to die for us, and to rise again within us. We do not go to God merely " as if He were our Father, " or to our fellow-men " as if they were our brothers, " just as Jesus did not act merely " as if " He were a man. Jesus became a man in very truth, establishing us in the condition of brothers in the most rigorous sense of the word. It is the destiny of all men not only to treat each other as brothers, but to be brothers in the truest sense and to live together the most authentic, closest family life.

Let us pause for an instant and consider this reality which seems so commonplace because we have not made it part of our lives. The fact is this: all men are called to be, together, children of the Father—the most degenerate as well as the most strong-willed, the most insignificant as well as the most influential, savages as well as the hyper-civilized, proud of the knowledge that has domesticated the forces of nature and discovered atomic energy. All without exception are called by Christ and His Church to be children of God, to live by the same spiritual heritage and the same grace, as children of the same family. All are utterly unworthy and incapable, by birth, of living the superhuman life offered them by God's totally gratuitous benevolence. And yet they are called by the Blessed Trinity to become, in union with one another, an entity at once very lowly and very splendid: a family of forgiven sinners.

Only at the moment of reconciliation do estranged parties understand wherein they have been at fault. We do not realize the evil of our sins until after we have been converted. We do not see how unworthy we are of the gratuitous invitation of divine love until we have accepted it. It is only when we have finally become aware of our destiny of grace that we grasp our indigence before God and become truly grateful and humble. And only when we see our misery in its starkness do we glimpse the existence of something above and beyond our wretchedness. Everything negative within us appears in its true light when juxtaposed to something positive. To have a Christian sense of sin we need to be aware of the vast universal mercy bestowed upon all of us. Then only can we go to God and to men, freed from self-love and bitterness, and with the souls of reconciled sons. We must go through this rigorous conversion in order to recognize both our weakness and our strength, to be really ourselves and really together, really united to our brothers.

And so all of us are equally indigent in the presence of the same mercy that works in all men in a way that often escapes the eye. We are equally naked, regardless of our natural endowments or importance, in the face of a destiny that is too great for us. We are all dependent upon a love given to us gratuitously, we are all in need of a forgiveness that will elevate us to a state above anything we have a right to hope for. The divine call to live, through grace, in union with God and neighbor, in a family whose bonds are forged by our community in sin and forgiveness, is evidently the most heart-stirring message of brotherhood men have ever heard or ever will hear.

The work of Redemption in the Church

God's fatherly plan will be consummated only in heaven, the homeland of unity. There we shall be united to Christ Jesus in a way that is beyond description here on earth; and in Him we shall be united to one another in an ineffable way, with which the closest human ties cannot remotely compare.

The Church is the mysterious realization of God's will to unity. It is an anticipation of the definitive success of the work of creation, a beginning of the total and permanent presence of men before God and of men to one another. It is the start here on earth of the eternal exchange in which men of every race, color, and culture will be a new people, a holy nation, the eternal kingdom of the risen Lord. It is the prelude to the fulfillment of our Savior's instant desire: " That all may be one, even as Thou, Father, in Me and I in Thee " (John 17:21).

The Church is the conclusion of the history of the world, a conclusion that is already present in a visible, yet hidden way. The God of Abraham, Moses, and Jesus Christ has always been, is now, and will be until the end of time, the hidden God. It was as a hidden God that He was present to His people in the days of the Old Covenant, and that He came to live among men during His earthly career as Savior. The only ones who recognized the Savior in the carpenter of Nazareth were those who saw Him with the eyes of faith. And only souls open to mystery can recognize Him now in His Church.

The divine work that will some day be consummated in the light unfolds here on earth through signs that indicate God and His action without revealing Him. That is the function of the sacraments, and of the Eucharist in particular, which is the center of the liturgy and of the whole life of the Church. For in the Eucharist the Lord shows believers they are destined for the communion of heaven, made possible by the mysterious efficacy of His death on the cross. In this sacrament He leads them toward eternal communion with Himself.

A member of the Church is a person who has been admitted through baptism to a participation in the Eucharistic mystery consummated in sacramental Communion, and admitted also to communion with the Mystical Body of Christ. The priesthood gives men power over the Eucharistic body of Jesus, and correlatively over His Mystical Body. The words by which the ecclesiastical hierarchy teaches and guides the Mystical Body are in a certain way the prolongation of the sacramental words that actualize the Eucharistic presence. The life of the Church, among priests and faithful, is the continuation of the Eucharist. The problem of the Church's vitality is the problem of sacramental Communion and of its continuation in the communion of charity.

The Church, which is the mystical prolongation of the Eucharistic presence of Jesus, is, like the Eucharist, a sign. It is an efficacious sign of the work of salvation whose dimensions will be revealed to us only in heaven. Just as the action of sacramental grace goes beyond the administration of the sacraments, so the action of the Holy Spirit who quickens the Church goes beyond the frontiers of the Church. The Church of today, the universal people committed by Christ to the work of saving the world, is the mysterious sign of God's action within all men without distinction of race or human worth. But it is still a preparation. Only in heaven, on the day of ultimate fulfillment, shall we realize in joyful wonderment the breadth and depth of this divine undertaking, whose imperfect instrument is the temporal Church.

Diversity in the service of unity within the Church

The Church is the unity of the end of time, anticipated in time. But the unity of heaven is not present upon earth like a diamond in a jewel-case, like a lifeless thing in an inert wrapping. It is like seed cast in a field that receives its adult plant structure both from the sun above and from the humus into which it plunges its roots, adapting itself to the soil whose impress it will retain even while refashioning it in its growing fibers. The unity for which God created the world has already taken root within it. During the course of time, it has acquired its timeless traits. That is the reason why God created time, and planted His Church in the soil of human history.

When the Church established her own spiritual unity among men, she did not ignore or underestimate the diversity of epochs and cultures. Nor did she ignore or underestimate the unities constantly being created, in the history of the world and of each individual, by work, friendship, family, and nation. The Church does not superimpose herself from the outside upon the multitude of earthly societies as if they were extraneous to the goal she is pursuing. Her role consists at once in being distinct from these communities and in being alive within them.

The mysterious unity that the Church realizes finds expression in her liturgy, her dogma, and her moral teaching, in the grouping of the faithful into communities within the Church such as dioceses, parishes, religious associations, as well as in the docility of believers to the authorities in charge of worship, dogma, moral teaching, and Christian institutions. And out of all this, out of belonging to the same Christ, surrender to the same Father, docility to the same Spirit, out of this identity of faith, hope, and charity, there comes into being a privileged— even though admittedly imperfect— way of living together. But the Church cannot limit herself to fulfillments that are strictly her own. She must also infuse her life of grace into purely human communities, and thus in a certain sense transfigure the unity they attain. She must elevate their goals of unity, without changing their intrinsic chatacteristics, to a level that is more than human.

Christian life has its own activities, such as public and private prayer, the study of revealed truth, the practice of asceticism. But obviously it does not limit itself to these things; nor does the unity of Christian life so limit itself. Christian living is not something added on to a man's job or to his family life, nor does it dispense a man from human action. It penetrates and quickens his human activities. Charity is not a quantity added on to the efforts of economists and jurists to bring agreement among men. It does not substitute its solutions for those provided by labor, medicine, social laws, and international treaties. Charity cannot and should not replace human procedures. On the contrary, it must penetrate and quicken them. Likewise, the Church is not superimposed from the outside on the labor community, the family, or the nation. Nor, except to fill the gap in exceptional circumstances, does she assume their tasks. Rather, she breathes life into them. She must do her part so that the family and the nation may be truly themselves, and so that men may live super-naturally as children of God in these human communities. She must nurture the unity of the home, the internal peace within and among nations, even while she is striving to attain a unity and peace that are supernatural gifts of God.

In her life-giving and unifying work, the Church must hold fast to a twofold realism. She must be attentive to both divine and human realities. The community in which the career of Christ is continued here on earth possesses as its own the treasures of faith and charity. And since these are the virtues of wayfarers, they are imbued with hope. But these virtues are lived within and according to a civilization. Everything relating to civilization also stems from God's plan, and hence is of concern to the Church and invites the efforts of Christians. The Church cannot be indifferent to the efforts of earthly societies toward unity. She cannot be indifferent to human progress. Nor is God any less interested in these things than is the farmer in the transformation of the soil where his wheat is growing.

The spiritual and the temporal

God is at work within the world at various levels and in countless ways. The simplest technical advance—even if it is only the discovery of a new textile fiber or the invention of a child's toy—provides a stepping stone for His supernatural work. Everything that makes civilization advance causes development in man's way of being a man and also in his manner of living with God. To make civilization progress is to give man an opportunity, directly or indirectly, of going to God with all that God has placed in him. Even things that have no directly favorable religious impact require the Christian's collaboration. The material world was also created by God, and we depend upon it in order to be ourselves. All earthly things are the concern of God's people, just as they are the Creator's concern. Faith in the God of heaven and earth, the one master of all things, obliges the believer to join with the non-believer in respecting temporal progress.

Just as God works at many levels in this world, so the

Church's tasks are very diverse. Some of her members, called to the priesthood and entrusted by God with a specific mission, are the appointed ministers of His sacraments and of His word. Others adopt a life organized around and sanctioned by the vows of religion, in order to consecrate themselves solely to prayer or to the service of their brothers. Still others dedicate themselves to the same goals without entering the religious state. The great majority are asked to perform, as Christians, the activities common to all men.

There is great diversity also in the ways in which the men whom God is leading to ultimate unity are actually brought together. It may come about through religious gatherings or Catholic Action, through Christian professional groups formed for the purpose of promoting the mode of life willed by Christ, through community services enlisting members of various faiths, through labor unions or business associations having nothing to do with religion, the family, or the state, through international societies, etc.

Everywhere, whether in the cloister or in the world, whether in the supernatural work of grace or in some secular endeavor, the sons and daughters of the Church must live by the same spirit, a spirit we shall now try to analyze.

The Christian's attachment and detachment

It is an oversimplification of Christianity to say that it detaches the Christian from all concern for bodily well-being, and focusses his attention on fidelity to the moral law. In truth, we are invited to an entirely different attitude. On the one hand, we are asked to take to heart the tasks of this world, and on the other to be detached even from our virtues. The expression " detachment from our virtues " may surprise us, but it describes a very important reality. It means that we may not have a proprietary attitude toward any good it may be our privilege to do. We may not look down with the scorn of the spiritually rich upon those who have vices. Nor, in the face of our own sins may we adopt the rancor of those who have failed. We are forbidden to be complacent in our successes or to yield to vexation in our defeats.

Complacency and bitterness are solitary attitudes which we may not cultivate. We must strive for thanksgiving and repentance, which are forms of love, attitudes of communion.

We must therefore do our best to obey the moral law, and yet be detached from the results of our efforts, humbly accepting the fact that we are nothing but poor sinners. We must strive manfully to succeed in our fight for purity, even though we clearly see the residue of impurity present even in the pure, of pride in the humble, and egoism in the charitable. The lifeblood of Christianity is not a more or less infantile nostalgia for purity. Its lifeblood consists of faith, hope, and charity, which teach us to know the heart of God and therefore to accept, without being resigned to it, the deceitfullness of our own heart.

The essential for us is not to change over from vice to virtue. For we can make this transition without becoming more detached from self, without being more filially abandoned to God, that is, without attaining true Christian virtue. Obviously, this is not a reason for giving up our efforts to be men of character. We must continue to strive, but with a different attitude, without satisfaction when we succeed or discouragement when we fall. And this demands a much more fundamental conversion than passage from vice to the haughty virtue of the Pharisee. The Jews were commanded to renounce their proprietary sentiments with regard to the spiritual riches of the Old Testament. These riches were given back, transfigured, to those who were willing to make the sacrifice. The others were alienated from God by their attachment to the gifts they had received from Him.

We must detach ourselves from everything that is not God, the personal God who is the only absolute value to which we must cleave without reservation. We must detach ourselves from everything else, without becoming indifferent to it. It is not true, therefore, that for us morality is the supreme value, and that all other goods seem negligible by comparison. Our attitude toward morality must be detached. That is to say, our soul must die to its own ambitions for moral perfection, even while being deeply committed to the effort to attain it. And the same applies to the other values in which we must take an interest in accordance with their relative importance, but with the same fundamental perspective.

This applies also to the progress of civilization and even to material progress. We cannot be indifferent to them, and yet we must remain detached from them. We are asked to fight against illness, while accepting the possibility of never attaining health; to battle poverty while remaining poor in spirit; to take an interest in culture even after we have renounced it; to combat injustice without rebelliousness; to be firm and yet kind, intransigent and in the same measure understanding, obedient and yet not subservient, active but not agitated; to speak with a soul steeped in silence; to be silent not out of unhealthy introspection but as a form of communion. What is demanded of us in all things is not violence, but a strength, whose criterion is meekness, and whose foundation is humility.

Death and resurrection in our response to divine love

We are asked to die to ourselves, so that God may live in us. In short, we are asked to love. And love always means dying to self, while living for another and by another. Love, therefore, always condemns us to a paradoxical attitude. Thus, when a man and wife are tempted to ask themselves whether they have gotten enough out of their marriage, they must turn the question around and ask themselves if they have given enough. For that is the law of love. We receive in the measure that we give, we possess ourselves in the measure that we lose ourselves, we become more ourselves in proportion to our renouncement of self.

To love is always to die to self by living a new life in which we regain whatever we have sacrificed through affection, enriched with new value. Human affection—whether it be friendship or conjugal love—involves a portion of physical attraction. But since this is a human affection and not merely an instinctive attachment, the physical factors are integrated into a superior synthesis, going through a kind of death and resurrection. Instinct is active in a noble conjugal love, but the life that quickens it is very different from pure instinct. Conjugal love is similarly transfigured when it is integrated into a spirituality of marriage. A Christian husband and wife who love God together with their whole souls and with all their strength do not love each other less, but in a different way.   Love of God does not bring death to their mutual affection, but death and resurrection.

The same is true of all the Christian's earthly interests. The paradoxical attitude demanded of him is not merely a matter of exercising balance as between care for his health and resignation to illness, between ambition to succeed in life and acceptance of defeat, between enthusiasm for intellectual pursuits and renouncement of culture, between fighting for justice and leniency toward enemies   Something very different from these impossible calculations is called for.   He is expected to see everything in a different light: to place himself in the presence not of things or ideas, but of Someone to be loved.   He is asked to believe in a love, and to accept an exchange of affection.   Such is the great conversion that will never be completed in our souls.

This supernatural conversion can be compared to what happens on the purely human level when, thanks to a great love, a man achieves an equilibrium that he had sought in vain through reason and interior monologues.   The paradoxical alloy of commitment and emancipation, of attachment and detachment, demanded of the Christian, can be achieved only if he breaks out of his solitude, enters into a communion and consents to a dialogue. A man left to his own resources is incapable of discerning and following the mode of behavior which the Gospel proposes to the believer.   It is a path that he can follow only with the God who, in His love, asks him to put his trust in Him through faith. Granted this condition, then the impossible is given.   The believer who is filially attached to his Father will be saved from the world that threatens to engulf him, and at the same time be present in this world from which he may have been tempted to withdraw in isolation.   His destiny is not a compromise between the spirit of the world and religious evasion.   The life of a family is not made up of compromise between selfishness and altruism. It consists of a higher unity, created by faith in a love and response to this love.

Christianity brings Someone into our lives, not merely abstract principles; its lifeblood is charity, not merely loyalty to an ideology.   That is why we can and must take part in all earthly tasks with a supernatural spirit.   Thus the hope we put in human effort will be transfigured, and instead of usurping the place of theological hope through which we reach up to God, it will be a form of theological hope.

Let us emphatically repeat: The Church is not of this world, and yet she is not extraneous to this world. We are citizens of another land, and yet part of earth's adventure in a different way than before. The reason we are in this paradoxical situation is that we are committed to a love. The only thing that really turns a life topsy-turvy is a presence or an absence, the presence or the absence of someone we love. God, who is love, is present in our lives, and as a result men are present to us in a new way.

Faith turns the believer's life topsy-turvy because it brings the living God into it, God the Father, Son, and Holy Spirit. And in placing the believer in the presence of the personal God, it places him in the presence of human persons. In the last analysis there is only one sin, and that is to deliberately ignore the living God, to willfully forget the Love who has given all things to us, and in consequence to treat God and men as things. In other words, there is only one sin, and that is the sin of willful solitude.

To enter the Church is to find God and men—in Christ, with Christ, and through Christ. The Church is not a philosophical society or an organization to help improve our moral life. She is that and much more besides. She is the continuation of Christ. The Church is an extension of Christ, who is a living paradox. He is man and God, He is one of us and His homeland is heaven. He was the God of holiness, and He became the son of a sinful race, living our sinful state integrally except for sin itself. He preached forbearance, but was intransigent with regard to sin. He suffered martyrdom, but changed this defeat into His supreme victory. He accepted death but triumphed over it, making it a passage to a new life. He overcame Satan by turning his own weapons against him, by bearing with us the yoke to which sin had condemned us. With Christ, the Church is a living paradox. In her, the human meets the divine, death meets life. In her, the Paschal mystery, the mystery of death and resurrection, is continued.

Docility to the Holy Spirit and participation in the mystery of death and resurrection lived by the Church

But we cannot solve all our problems merely by rediscovering what the Church is, by returning into the presence of the personal God, the Triune God, the One who makes us die and makes us live, by seeing the context of reality in the light of these truths.

We are not dispensed from our obligation to reflect and choose simply because God has made Himself known to us through His Revelation and given us clear-cut rules of conduct for salvation through the voice of the Church. Life is given us so that we may use it inventively. We know our ultimate goal, but we must all join forces and blaze the trail to it together. We must march forward in union with the Church.

The Gospel tells us how we should use the goods of this world or agree to do without them. It does not say in what measure one or another of us may amass wealth or get rid of what he possesses. The Gospel teaches us in what spirit we should consider sickness, but does not tell how far we should go in using one or another means of combatting it. It teaches us the attitude we should have toward injustice, but does not say to what extent we must endure it or stop it in certain concrete circumstances.

The spirit of poverty, whether it is applied to our virtues, our intellectual gifts, or our material goods, obviously demands a certain degree of renunciation. Otherwise it would be impossible for us to use the things of this world as if we were not using them. We must reserve certain hours exclusively for God, in order to maintain a spirit of prayer at other times. We need to accept humiliations in order to defend our rights with humility. We must give a part of our riches in order to administer the rest as stewards of God's property. The Church likewise needs souls exclusively consecrated to God, so that their influence may help others to remain faithful to the Lord. There must be men in the Church who assume the social function of seeking perfection, so that the desire for perfection may burn brightly in all the members of the Christian community. Each one must recognize the path into which the Holy Spirit is leading him, and rediscover it in the choices he must make day by day. To answer this vocation is not merely to answer an individual call. It is to cooperate with God's plans for the whole community, in which He assigns a special place and a particular role to each one.

God puts us face-to-face with a question; the faith we have professed in Him obliges us to seek an answer. All believers and the Church as a whole are faced with a question and must seek an answer. In the Church, which is one, different roads are open. Some are called to found a family, to support it and make it prosper by using the material goods at their disposal. Others are called to renounce family and material goods, and to embrace the religious state. The Gospel does not specify which of us must get married and which must enter religion, or the amount of material comfort a married man must strive to give his family. The Gospel simply tells us in what spirit we are to pursue our earthly careers or make the vows of poverty, chastity, and obedience.

This spirit is unique. The Sermon on the Mount speaks to all disciples of Christ. The same spiritual impetus must quicken the Christian layman in his trade or profession as the nun in her cloister. In order to discern the concrete deeds demanded by fidelity to this approach to life we need supernatural judgment born of a well-balanced temperament, but even more of holiness.

No one can hear the Holy Spirit if he isolates himself. For He is the Spirit of a family, of the Trinitarian life in heaven and of the Church on earth. It is our task, in the unfolding of history, to work with our feet firmly planted on earth and our hearts in heaven. And this task is not given to us as isolated individuals but to the community, at once of earth and heaven, that is the Church. No one can judge what the spirit of his own vocation demands of him unless he is attentive to the diverse spiritual inspirations present in the great Christian family in which he lives.

Within the Church, the hierarchy must safeguard God's revealed message and maintain the faithful in a supernatural attitude. Jesus entrusted to the Twelve, under the headship of Peter, the faith by which His Church was to live. He entrusted to them the guidance of His flock and the task of teaching them how to apply God's immutable commands to changing circumstances. It is the hierarchy's function to interpret the word of God and to organize the means best adapted to the fulfillment of

God's plan of death and resurrection. For example, the hierarchy must lend its support to efforts for greater social justice without approving the class struggle; it must be receptive to the concept of nationality without encouraging nationalisms; and it must promote whatever can assure greater happiness on earth while constantly reminding man that he was not created for the happiness of earth.

To acquit itself of this task in accordance with God's Will, the hierarchy needs to carry on a dialogue with the entire Christian community. For example, it was the Marian devotion of the ordinary faithful that guided Church authorities in discovering the mind of God with regard to the Blessed Virgin Mary and her role. Had there not been this popular movement, inspired by the Holy Spirit, among the faithful, the taught Church, it is probable that we would not have had the definition of the dogma of the Assumption by the teaching Church. If there had not been Christian homes where the spirituality of the family was nurtured, the doctrine of the Church on marriage would certainly be much poorer. If Christian laymen and laywomen had not labored in the domain of social action, the Church would not have the social doctrine she teaches today. Morever, in its teaching, the hierarchy does not solve the concrete family and social problems facing the laity. It sets forth the question facing the Church, clarifies its terms, thus placing the obligation on persons and groups—families, nations, social classes—to seek a solution. The life of the Church consists in cooperation and exchange of views between the hierarchy and the faithful, as well as between individual persons and the various communities to which they belong.

It is the same Holy Spirit who guides the teaching Church and the taught Church conjointly. The same Spirit guides the whole Church in order to accomplish within her a work of death and life—and hence a work of unity. And this work is not primarily the task of the hierarchy in which the laity collaborate, but the common good of the entire risen people, i.e., of all Christians. The same docility to the God of holiness is required of all, if He is to act in them; but it is required of each one according to his own specific function. Part of the Christian way of living the mystery of salvation together consists in the obedience that God demands to the authority that He Himself has instituted. This is one of the essential concrete forms of death to self. Obedience in the spirit of faith does not exclude initiative or suppress freedom of expression. In fact it requires them, but on condition that remarks made to superiors be inspired by submission to the God of holiness—the same God who speaks inwardly to each one of us and also through authority. Obedience requires that any steps taken be inspired not by mere human wisdom, but by death to self impelled by charity.

The habitual disposition requisite for participation in the Paschal mystery of the Lord is a climate of prayer. The soil where conscious and explicit prayer germinates is peace born of meekness, good will, and humility. This profound and faithful way of receiving God and men, is the way of the poor in spirit who know divine love has lavished its favors on them and who expect this love to transform their lives. It is what might be called a " prayer of attitude. " It is a lived prayer that becomes conscious whenever an opportunity arises to place the soul in God's presence. This " habitual prayer " is fashioned during moments of formal prayer, and conversely it gives these moments depth and sincerity.

The habitual disposition to participate in the Paschal mystery is the overflowing of the Eucharistic mystery into the life of the Church. In all their activities, the leaders and members of the Christian community are as inseparable as are the laity and the priest during the celebration of Mass. We shall point out one aspect of this collaboration, required in the Eucharistic prayer as well as in all Christian effort. In order to distribute Communion efficaciously, the priest who is in the service of Christian life needs someone to receive the Eucharist into his life. And this presupposes a virile preparation and a noble effort on the communicant's part to prolong the effects of his Communion. The Christian is a man who lives from one Communion to the next, never ceasing to be a member of the Body of the Church.

The apostolate of the Church

After this brief sketch of the life of the Church, let us discuss her apostolic mission.

Obviously God can accomplish, without man, the work to which He invites him. For example, God can make us understand by a simple illumination of the intellect what He prefers to teach us through the words of others. God can get along without our efforts to save the world. He could have saved it without the Church, just as He could have saved it without Christ, without the Incarnation of the Word, and without His Passion and Resurrection.

But God who created the universe with a view to its ultimate unity in Christ, has willed to save us by uniting us in Christ even here on earth. He created us in order to gather us together again in heaven; and it pleases Him to see us together already here on earth, in our love for Him and in our fraternal effort to get those around us to love Him. He seems to be eager to see us together, and He wants our road here on earth to bear the seal of the unity that will exist at the end of the journey. This mark of unity in our world is the Church.

Since the career of the Church is the continuation of Christ's, it is apostolic in its very essence. The Christian community perpetuates Jesus' union with His Father. Our Savior's deepest concern has been entrusted to us: His desire that His Father shall become our Father. The apostolate entrusted to the Christian family is a form of filial loyalty. We must sacrifice ourselves for God in the Church because we know how eminently He deserves to be known and loved, because we repeat after Jesus the fundamental prayer that expresses the whole meaning of our lives as believers: " Our Father, who art in heaven, hallowed be Thy name; Thy kingdom come; Thy will be done on earth as it is in heaven. " The apostolate is simply the *Our Father* absorbed into our lives.

Apostolic zeal, in the believer as in Christ Himself, is fundamentally directed to the glory of the Father rather than to the salvation of men. Here again, it is not a matter of juxtaposing two attitudes of soul but of uniting them into a single attitude that is at first glance paradoxical. It might seem that loving others for the love of God is not really loving them for themselves. We do not love someone for himself when we love him out of principle. But the situation is completely different when we are united to someone through the meditation of a personal presence, beloved by ourselves and by the one we love. To clarify this point, let us take an example from family life. We love our nephews and nieces far more than the children of unknown parentage to whom we may be generously devoting our time and effort. We love the children of our brothers and sisters precisely because they are the children of our brothers and sisters. And the presence of the parents, far from making us love their children less for their own sakes, makes our contact with them much more personal. The same is true of the believer in whom love for the Father awakens the spirit of brotherhood.

Christ is the Mediator not because He is halfway between God and men, but because He is, in the unity of a single person, truly God and truly man; and thus He is at once as close to the Father and as close to men as it is possible to be. Now Christ's mediation is continued in us; and we shall be genuinely dedicated to our fellow men in the measure that we are dedicated to the God who shares His life with us.

The apostolate demands both love of God and love of men. And at the same time, it presupposes a sense of God and a sense of sin, an awareness of what the Most High is and an awareness of our own indigence which He alone can fill. It is very different, therefore, from a purely human work of education or propaganda, in that it is rooted in adoration. Before altruism and philanthropy can be transmuted into apostolic action, they must pass through a death and a resurrection. Death and resurrection are the essential conditions of the apostolic life, as of Christian life in general.

The apostle must stand before the living God, acknowledge in a spirit of faith that this God deserves the sacrifice of all things to Him, so that He may accomplish His life-giving work in him—all things, including the desire to do some good. And then this desire will be transfigured by true charity. We must renounce, for the sake of God, our natural ambition to influence others, so that this ambition may be transformed into apostolic zeal. We must accept theologically the fact that we are good for nothing, in order to become supernaturally good for anything. On the other hand, we cannot yield to natural inertia or discouragement. We must die to these forms of egocentricity, in order to engage in our apostolic work, sure of God as only sons can be.

To be an apostle is at once to intervene and to stay in the

background. It is not a question of wanting others to be what we desire, even if these desires are noble, or what they desire to be, even if their desires are very idealistic. It is wanting them to be what God desires, out of love for Him.

The work to be done in the Church for God is also accomplished by God, for only God can give God. " No one can come to Me," says Christ, " except the Father ... draw him" (John 6: 44). And St. Paul teaches that no one can acknowledge Jesus as Lord unless the Holy Spirit make this profession of faith within him. The supernatural influence of the Church can only be that of the Holy Spirit acting through her. We can have a truly spiritual influence only by accepting the grace that permeates us. We are asked to be receptive to God's action so that, through us, it may be contagious. We must die to ourselves so that God may live in us and accomplish His work through us.

Even though God could do His work of divinization without us, and though it is more His than ours, it is still truly our work. It would be false to say that God accomplishes good on the occasion of our actions and not through them. Just as the sacraments really cause grace, we too, in God's hand, are real causes of what is done through us, and not merely occasions.

God wants to achieve the unity of the universe through the charity we have for one another, drawing us to Himself through one another, and saving all of us together. Jesus died so that His Church in heaven might be the universe eternally unified, so that His Church on earth might proclaim His Gospel to every creature. The words we believe in are addressed to the whole human race; the object of our hope is not merely our own personal destiny but the completion of Christ and the fulfillment of His prayer for unity.

The Church owes it to herself to work in many different ways to help the world attain this unity. It is incumbent upon her to promulgate the message and to make sure it penetrates deep into the lives of Christians. At the same time, she must be attentive to all that can prepare the way for grace. And that is why she must encourage every civilizing effort of man. On the other hand, while the propagation of the Gospel is first of all a supernatural work whose power lies in prayer, it requires organi-

zation, techniques for the diffusion of ideas, and the use of all
legitimate human means.

The apostolate and the Christian life

Whatever its form, the apostolate always retains its fundamental
character. It is not primarily an enterprise or a strategy. It is the
vitality of the Church. And in each apostle, it is the vitality of
his communion with Christ in the Church.

The Church—Christ living in us, accomplishing a work
of life and unity in us—is not solely a means of salvation. It *is*
salvation, the object of our hope already realized in a certain way.
The Church is at once means and end, just as a human community
is not simply a means we use in order to be men, but also a way of
being men. Nor is the apostolate merely a means of helping
others to attain salvation. It is the Christian way of living our
salvation: living it together. To be an apostle is to seek God,
and therefore to be concerned about our neighbor. It is not to
recruit adherents to an ideology; it is to bring others, more or less
directly, into the presence of Someone by the very fact that we
ourselves live in His presence.

It has been said that the education of children is first of all
the education of their parents. We educate only in educating
ourselves. The same is true of the apostolate. For it implies
above all else a tireless effort on the part of the apostle
to convert himself; it presupposes such a conversion and also
produces it.

Fraternal assistance is not an activity added onto family
life; it is one of its forms. Mutual aid among friends is not
an activity added onto friendship. And for the Christian, the
apostolate is not an occupation superimposed upon his Christian
life. True, mutual aid can place excessive burdens on those
bound by ties of family or friendship. The apostolate likewise
may demand additional work of believers aware of their brothers'
needs. Even so, mutual aid in a family and the apostolate in the
Church are not restricted to this. The apostolate is not a work
of supererogation added onto the Christian life, or simply a part

of this life. The apostolate is above all else a way of living the Christian life.

An apostolic life is essentially the life of a child of the Father, and therefore of a son of the Church. Anyone who accepts all the realities of his daily life in the spirit of the *Our Father*, who faces each day in relation to the personal God whose fatherly love leavens the universe, who strives to live by the faith we have just described, will always remain in the climate of apostolic action. To the extent that we face our daily tasks with a more Christian attitude, with the souls of sons and brothers, we shall help others, by the very way we do things, to know the God we believe in; we shall make those around us more aware of His presence. But if we live in this manner, we shall shoulder new burdens and find time for labors exclusively in the service of Christianity. At the same time, these apostolic labors will often lead us to the discovery of the mode of Christian living best suited to every phase of our state of life.

The extent to which we devote our days to apostolic tasks, granted the conditions of our state of life, will be one of the criteria of the spiritual quality of our lives. And the way we fulfill our duty of state will also be one of the marks of the sincerity of our commitment to apostolic works.

We must not confuse " work in organizations " with being an apostle. The important thing is to " live, " to live a filial and fraternal life amid the work of various organizations. In this connection we should realize that we can make a greater contribution to the reunion of men in God without taking on any more activities than if we didnt have faith, provided we do whatever we are doing in a different way. This can make terrible demands on a Christian. Conversely, we can spend ourselves in a multitude of Christian activities and yet not have a Christian spirit, or a true understanding of apostolic action. This is a real danger to anyone who devotes himself to a cause.

Docility to the Holy Spirit in the apostolate

How much of our life must we devote to these various tasks? To what extent must we act or abstain from action, have recourse to human means or to prayer? The Gospel does not give us any specific answers, but it does state the apostolic spirit with which we should live our life as Christians and utilize earthly modes of action: namely, the spirit of humility and supernatural trust, which is the spirit of prayer and the opposite of the will to power. The Gospel also tells us how we must pray: with a spirit of filial trust and not the sullen scorn of one who seeks refuge in God because he has lost confidence in men. It does not tell us what we must do to collaborate with non-believers. It merely says that the most important thing is to live with them as brothers, without any superiority complex attributed to right-thinking persons.

The question the individual believer must answer must also be answered by the Church. To what extent must the Church at any moment in history—and notably at the moment in which we live—devote herself to missionary activity, or commit her vital resources to the evangelization of areas of the world where she has long been present? To what extent must she encourage human efforts at civilization and urge Christians to take part in them, or turn the attention of believers exclusively to spiritual needs? How far should she go in using earthly techniques of power, or renounce them and urge men to prayer and sacrifice? The Gospel gives no specific answer to these questions. But it does say categorically that we must never sacrifice the truth to the demands of the moment, that we must use human means with complete detachment, or, if we renounce human means, to do so in a spirit of faith and not with bitterness or contempt.

To answer these questions, to pose them to Christians in a precise and exacting way, the Lord has given His Church official teachers and placed the spiritual apostolate in their hands. This mission was entrusted to St. Peter and his bishops; and they in turn called other men to this work, by administering the sacrament of holy orders to them. But the laity also join in this task which belongs to the community as a whole. Their support is needed by the clergy, who are inadequate in numbers to carry on this immense work. By living their laymen's life in a truly fraternal way, they can exert influence on others and bear witness in their own way to Christ and His Gospel.

God has given the Church her hierarchy to coordinate the

apostolic action in which the laity are called to participate. He
has given her the hierarchy so that there might be an exchange
of life, thought, and generosity between clergy and laity for the
sake of the apostolate.

The spirit of faith in the life of the Church and of each member of the Church

It has not been our purpose to describe in detail the specific
task of the laity in the Church, or to explain the bonds that unite
them to their leaders in the supernatural life. We have sought
merely to call to mind the vistas of faith that should inspire
our reflections on God's plan for the present-day world and
for the Church of today, reflections that should be at once humble
and ambitious. What conclusion have we reached?

In great measure, each one of us must formulate his own
conclusion, in the presence of God. We must also reach it
together, in a spirit of docility to authority. Certainly we should
acknowledge that we lack a genuine apostolic sense, because our
horizons are too narrow, because we refuse to shoulder the
problems of others, the problems of the world, and of the Church.
Certainly we must try to understand once again that we are
called not only to act, but to live by the surnatural life; that to
live means " to live with "; that the apostolate is essentially a
life of sons and brothers called into being by a death and a
resurrection. Because of our failure to live the mystery of death
and resurrection which is the essential mystery of salvation
through the Church, we are in danger of unduly limiting our
objectives, of mistakenly wanting to be God's attorneys or business
representatives instead of His children. And for the same reason,
when we speak of the spirit of childhood we are in danger of
forgetting that this is not a sentimental and inoffensively
idealistic attitude, but a practical, lucid, and courageous stand
that will be more demanding in proportion to our charity.

We must relearn how to live together in our parishes, our
organizations, our families, and our neighborhoods. We must
relearn how to look upon men at opposite poles from us as our
close friends, because all men were present in the intention

of the dying Christ, in His will to save the world that gave birth
to the Church.

In thus rediscovering our Christianity, we shall become
aware of the Christian approach we must take to human values
as we perform the duties of our state of life, and to the human
values imbedded in all of man's efforts toward civilization and
progress.

The Church of God is imperfect, and we may be inclined
to focus our attention on these imperfections. Only in heaven
shall we understand her full splendor. We know that Christ
died for this Church whose misfortunes and defeats sometimes
disconcert us, for this Church which is our Mother. That should
suffice to quiet our anxiety and to give us confidence in prayer.
But it also requires us not to resign ourselves to situations which
a true spirit of faith cannot tolerate, to things that must be extir-
pated or amended, first and above all in ourselves.

We have believed in the love of our personal God for us,
and we have accepted it. We have believed in the Father who
draws us to Himself, in the Son who redeems us, and in the
Holy Spirit who dwells in our hearts. We have believed in
the God who is, who was, and who comes to us in His Church.

PART THREE

TASKS THAT MUST SUCCEED

V The Christian's interest in temporal progress

A few questions

Can the Christian who is honest with himself sincerely disclaim any interest in the goods of this world and in temporal progress? The norm of his value judgments must be the relationship of each of his activities to his last end, i. e., the possession of God. How can he, therefore, attach any value to the satisfactions of this world, to technical advances, scientific discoveries, and cultural triumphs when all these things seem as likely to hinder his search for the good as to serve it, and are therefore alien by nature to the moral order? In relation to man's last end, can science and culture have anything to offer besides a possible contribution to apologetics?

And do not the tenets of psychology agree with those of logic in this matter? For is it possible to sincerely want God, and God alone, while taking a deep interest in some earthly undertaking? Conversely, can we devote ourselves wholeheartedly to temporal tasks if we are convinced that the essential lies elsewhere and that these tasks are secondary?

In fact, did not Christ and the disciples who followed most closely in His footsteps insist, sometimes very rigorously, on the necessity of detachment, on the indifference to the world requisite for the soul's unimpeded ascent toward God? And does not history for its part show that improvement in living conditions weakens spiritual aspirations, and progress in civilization brings with it a decline in religion?

Besides, Christians eager to live their faith deeply are sometimes ill-at-ease in the exercise of their many purely human

functions. They may have the impression of being slaves to a
mode of life that can never be more than half-Christian, of being
obliged by their state of life to pay only half-hearted attention
to God's invitations. When they read certain pages of the
Gospel or compare their way of life with the cloister, their
condition as men committed to earthly tasks may seem to be made
up of compromises, and to imply a lack of logic and courage.

Some unbelievers think along the same lines. Certain
popular writers say that the Christian faith is an escape. To
expect a life beyond the grave, they claim, is to deny the ugliness
of this life and to diminish its authentic joys. And certain
Marxist authors are currently reproaching us for not being fully of
this world, for being incapable, for example, of sensing the
tragedy of the workers' plight, and for losing because of our
faith a part of the power for action and accomplishment we could
devote to present needs if we saw no future beyond it.

It is true that only the spiritual salvation of humanity counts
in the Christian destiny, and that a believer may be interested
in social progress for its own sake only insofar as it may have
religious repercussions? How can the attitude of Christians
interested in social questions be justified except as a forced
concession to the weakness of those who must be coaxed toward
eternity by whatever path is practicable for them, without asking
of them a renouncement of earthly goods that they could not
accept? Is not the Church's position, therefore, merely a matter
of opportunism or even of calculated propaganda? And is it
not true that even the most active Christian social reformers
can commit only a part of themselves to their work? For does
not their faith deprive them of the keenness of vision and innovating boldness of realistic revolutionaries who are completely
engrossed with concrete situations and free from metaphysical
phantasies as well as religious prejudice?

Adhering to reality in all its forms

While the Church has always encouraged the practice of the
evangelical counsels, she has steadfastly refused to follow the
extremists who wanted to prohibit the Christian from using the

things of the world. She has condemned them not only for their lack of moderation and sense of values, but in the name of the fundamental principles that govern her teaching.

The Christian knows that everything he is and has comes from God, and that the whole of creation is destined to return to God, its Author, in a spirit of love. Our duty here on earth is not merely to love with all our strength the One for whom we were made, but to love Him well. Not only does He ask us to love Him, He asks us to love Him by developing all our faculties and talents.

Assuming that two Christians love God equally—if we may be permitted to use quantitative terms in dealing with realities of the moral order—then a well-educated Christian has greater value before God than a Christian savage. Besides, if the savage's love is genuine, it will tend to grow not only in intensity but in human richness. Theological charity will inspire the uneducated faithful to seek enlightenment for his intellect, to refine the delicacy of his heart. It will impel him to adorn his loyalty to the Lord with all possible human perfection, it will start him on the road to civilization. The apostle will intuitively follow the same inspiration. In his zeal to bring men to God he will labor to make them more complete men. He will work to develop all their God-given aptitudes that can help them reach God through the harmonious and well-balanced efforts of a rich and integrated personality.

The world in which God has placed us is one of His languages, complementing the language of Scripture. The whole of reality, the work of the Creator who never turns His eyes away from it and maintains it in existence, bears witness to His expectations and intentions, and tells us His thoughts. In order to interpret the language spoken by the material world around us, we need the written word of the sacred books and the living word of the Church commenting on them. But we would misunderstand divine Revelation if we refused to accept the truths inscribed in the whole of creation, that the Church has taken under her tutelage through her commentary on the natural law.

The service of God is not an escape mechanism. On the contrary, it is the sheerest realism. The Church does not raise us to a higher level of existence by offering us an escape from the

problems that torment us—as music and poetry may be expected
to do.   The Church elevates us by showing us how to face the
circumstances that disconcert us and the difficulties that impede
our progress; by enabling us to understand and control our
human condition.   Loyalty to God stimulates our "sense of
reality."   We must be faithful to reality in all its forms in order
to be completely faithful to grace.

Too often, alas, we set God apart from the real world instead
of seeing Him present within it, instead of understanding men
and things through Him.   And because we place God outside
the world, we put the world in God's place.   To love God is to
love everything He gives us to love, and to make use of all the
capacities and talents He has given us in the service of love.

To love God in very truth is to love all our brothers in Him.
To love them as Christians is not to love them for the love of
someone who is extraneous to them, out of affection for another.
It is to love them because of what is most profoundly and nobly
themselves, namely, the divine presence within them.   It is to
love them also with every resource at our disposal, with all our
faculties for sympathy and understanding, with every means
available to us for being of service to them.

To love God effectively is to answer the voice whose echo
comes to us from the material world.   To accept temporal tasks
as Christians is not to submit to them because of reasons extrinsic
to them, but to take an interest in them for their own sakes.   The
Christian spirit must make us respect and even love the labors
entrusted to us.   We would be stopping midway in God's service
if we were to do work half-heartedly, if we were to acquiesce
in sentiments that keep us from devoting ourselves to our work
with our whole will, indeed, with our whole self.   Our ideal must
not be to perform out of a sense of duty work we refuse to enjoy,
but to accomplish with joy the work that duty demands of us.

If we do not aspire to this integration of our whole being
in our actions, we shall leave unused a portion of the capacities
God has given us.   We shall be refusing, more or less consciously,
more or less directly, to redirect to the Lord one or another
of the ways of knowing and loving Him that He has implanted
in us.   And such a refusal is a failure to see the unity intrinsic
in the idea that God created each of us and all things so that we

might return to Him all that we are and all that He has put into our hands.

In heaven shall be face-to-face with God, without any intermediary. On earth we are face-to-face with His works, and must be united to Him through them. We too often treat God as if He were an abstraction, and try to reach Him solely by way of abstract concepts, disregarding all the concrete realities that surround us and the concrete reality that we are. That is why flimsy wishes often replace firm determination in our lives. We would like to attain this or that ideal, we know very well what we would do if we were in certain favorable circumstances other than those in which Providence has placed us. We delude ourselves with " if's, " instead of resolutely fighting for the things it is our duty to want, and accepting the facts of our situation. We are so engrossed with things that do not exist, with our regrets and dreams, that we forget to listen to the divine message hidden under the humble and deceiving appearances of the present moment. We do not recognize God's very concrete invitation, extended to us through the commonplaces of each passing day.

We give too little attention to concrete things and too little respect to persons because we do not live in God's presence as we should. We would have much greater insight into the problems of our epoch and take a more active approach to them if we were deeply aware that the Lord is not an outsider to anything, and that everything deserves our interest because it is of interest first of all to Him. Our faith should not make us strangers to the world, but make us feel very close to it. It must not tear us away from reality, but plunge us into it, so that we may find God in it, with all the wealth of understanding made possible by His action outside of us and within us.

Everything within us can be a means of loving better, of loving more fully, with the plenitude of our human capacities. This includes our talents, our gifts of intellect and heart, and also our infirmities and faults, which we must not only endure but use or amend insofar as we are able. For then we can offer God a love nourished with everything He has placed within us, a love that will have the unity of our personality. God does not want a vague, nebulous love from us; He wants us to give Him every fiber of our concrete being. Perhaps He asks the affection of a sensitive and delicate soul, developed in the serenity of faith, and in the zest of hope and charity. Or He may want the affection of a passionate and choleric man who generously uses every natural and supernatural means to become meek and humble of heart.

Everything outside ourselves can be a means of loving better: the pleasurable as well as the useful, opportunities for relaxation as well as aids to recollection. To reach God, we must use everything that can help, including improved living conditions and progress in the arts and sciences. If we were more completely engrossed with God, we would more quickly discover how the things around us can help us and our brothers. We would take a deeper interest in the various scientific disciplines and advances in technology, in the many ways man can make profitable use of matter. Then we would be more complete men, and more completely men of our time.

Because our religious life lacks vigor, it remains on the periphery of our real life; and because it is isolated from our other activities, it is anemic. If we were more thoroughly Christian we would have a keener insight into the providential meaning of work, the family, and social life. Our human sensibilities would be richer, our intellect more alert, our will more docile and tenacious. If we were more deeply committed to our role as men, if we tried harder to see what the Lord expects of us in the secular world, our Christianity would be less of a sham.

Christian faith imposes other obligations on the believer besides religious duties. If the world is to move toward God, it must include other activities besides prayer. If men are to live together in charity, something besides charity is needed. For example, there have to be business relations, economic agreements, social action. To establish peace among peoples, it is not enough to ask for it, or even to propagate the spirit of the Gospel through unrealistic preaching; it is necessary that questions of techniques and procedures be solved in the spirit of understanding and mutual respect characteristic of the Gospel. Christians who want charity to triumph must shoulder their responsibilities in every endeavor in which charity becomes incarnate.

In the concrete world where God has placed us to serve Him, there are other problems besides those of religion, and they have repercussions on the life of faith. The entire universe comes from God, no less than Revelation. The Christian must respect the laws written by God in this universe, just as he does the laws promulgated by His Church.

The relative autonomy of natural values

The ideal, therefore, is to harmonize nature and the supernatural in the unity of Christian life. Everything in the world should enhance the way we belong to God—the use of inanimate objects, physical training, the enrichment of our emotions and intellect, economic activity and social progress. But since this is not always the case, is it permissible for the Christian to concern himself with forms of human progress even though they do not benefit his religious life?

Faith allows him to devote himself to science. It even invites him insistently to do so, because it tells him that his reason has been given him by God so that he may find God, and that science will make it possible for him to believe more deeply, more intelligently. But does faith permit the Christian to dedicate himself to science for its own sake, and to collaborate scientifically with atheists in a world where science will bear no fruit for religion? Does science for its own sake, solely as human knowledge, have any value according to Christian doctrine? And do technical and social progress deserve consideration, apart from any link they may have with the spiritual life? The question posed at the beginning of this book is still far from solved by what we have said.

So far, we have reflected on the consequences of the doctrine of creation. We must also remember other teachings of the Church along the same lines. The Church has refused to commit herself to the pessimism of those who deny all natural goodness to human acts unrelated to the order of grace. She does not admit that original sin has perverted nature to the point of depriving activities, proceeding solely from nature, of all value. Since that is the Church's dogma, what does theology teach concerning the relative autonomy this dogma recognizes in principle to natural values?

According to moral doctrine, certain activities are intrinsically evil. They are wrong by their very nature, and hence objectively condemnable, even if in certain cases they are done because of erroneous views or with a good intention. Such, for example, is the case of the murder of an innocent person. The act is evil in itself, even if performed with noble intentions. The distinction between objective and subjective morality applies also to good acts. A religious act, of its nature directed to God, may be performed less for God than against one's neighbor. Thus an action, in itself praiseworthy, is made loathsome by the perversity of the subject.

In judging the goodness of an act, we must distinguish not only between its objective morality and the subjective dispositions of its author. We must also note that the nature of an intrinsically evil act is not changed by the circumstances under which it is performed; whereas an act, good in itself, may be vitiated objectively because of the context in which it is performed. For example, recreation which in itself contributes to man's mental balance becomes objectively wrong when, in a given civilization, it takes on undue importance. For in its objective tenor it is no longer a human value. Again, a technological invention or a more efficient organization of labor, useful in themselves to man, may become objectively wrong if, instead of liberating him, they contribute to his enslavement. Such advances do not deserve the name of progress. In the abstract they remain desirable, but in the concrete they are pernicious.

Whatever helps man to fulfill himself as man is objectively adapted to help him attain more perfect harmony with his God. Whatever assures man a more human life can make his life as a Christian richer. The believer will call unreservedly good only activities directed toward God in a spirit of faith. But he will acknowledge authentic value in every human accomplishment that can help make man's return to God more perfect.

It would seem fitting therefore to distinguish between the ability of an activity or thing to help man come closer to God, and the use to which it is put. Whatever possesses this capacity is of value to the Christian and deserves his time and effort. Everything is worthy of the believer's interest, even though not objectively directed to God, if it offers man the opportunity of serving Him better. Whatever can establish closer contact between man and the One for whom he was created possesses, by reason of this fact, a dignity of its own. This is true of secular labors and of the temporal progress they accomplish. These are potentially means of serving God better. For Christians they are in fact such means; but for atheists, they remain unrelated to man's last end, as consciously envisaged. Regardless of the various attitudes of the individual men who use them, these means have value in their own right.

Human activities that have objective value are of two sorts. Some lead to God by their very nature, i.e., religious activities, although in practice they may not achieve their purpose through the fault of the persons performing them. Then there are activities which, in themselves, are merely capable of improving man's way of going to God, i.e., activities of a strictly secular nature. In certain cases the latter will contribute effectively to man's living closer to God. In others, they will remain extraneous to this search. But whether purely human values have an influence on religion or not, they do have meaning for Christian morality because of their possible orientation to man's last end.

Christian doctrine, therefore, need not ignore temporal progress. Certain improvements in the human conditions of life approved by natural law are also approved in principle by supernatural moral teaching. Such improvements do not involve any direct relationship with God, independently of the subject's dispositions in using them. And yet, in their objective structure, they are positively " in potency " to His service. Whether they become so in fact depends on the faith of the men who use them. They have been put in our power by God, to help us go to Him in the most harmonious and perfect way possible. This is true not only of their origins but of the ultimate purpose to which they can be directed. That is why the Creator gives them to us, and why they deserve the respect of every Christian.

Because we are Christians we must esteem all the means that can help man to improve his lot by the light of his natural reason. Because we are part of the supernatural order, we must remain resolutely loyal to natural values. The conquests of science and advances in man's social well-being are values in themselves, independently of any effective contribution they may make to religious life. They merit the Christian's interest by themselves, apart from any consideration of apologetics or apostolic conquest.

At a time when it is so urgent that men be brought to God, it is legitimate for the Church, therefore, to encourage some priests and religious to abandon all ambition to participate in direct Christian action, and devote themselves instead to science or manual labor. For in so doing they are serving the Church indirectly, as are all who contribute in some way to the betterment of man. They also manifest the value inherent in all human work, as recognized by the Church, thus contributing to a better understanding of the Church and to making God better known and loved.

The tasks of the Church and the tasks of Christians

The Church does not usually shoulder purely human responsibilities except in case of emergency or to meet the needs of charity. It cannot be otherwise. Even though all human undertakings can, and according to God's desire, must contribute to a richer supernatural life, only spiritual works in the strict sense are part of the Church's mission and under her jurisdiction. While spiritual works are exclusively within the province of the Church, secular tasks are within the domain of temporal society whose autonomy the Church recognizes. There are overlapping areas, of course, which concern both religious and civil society. In such areas, the Church asks for an opportunity to cooperate with the state. Then there is work to be done by individual citizens or groups of citizens, and not directly by the state, but which the state must respect and encourage. Christians have the right to want to do this work in a Christian climate and through religious organizations. The Church for her part defends this right of her faithful. She encourages activities that her children carry on in comparative independence of both state and Church in organizations that are truly Christian even though not officially a part of the Church.

There are many tasks to be done in humanity's march toward God. The Church must do her own work, while lending support to other efforts that have a value of their own and may have repercussions on religion. The Church takes an interest in social questions for two reasons: first, because of the importance of these problems in themselves, and the value of safeguarding the rights of the individual; secondly, because of the influence social phenomena have on the religious progress of humanity at this time. But she does not assume the responsibility of solving these problems. She leaves to the state and to individual citizens the tasks that are theirs. In fact some have insisted so much on the limitations the Church places on her teaching as to claim that there is no such thing as a " social doctrine of the Church. "

Obviously the tasks of the faithful have wider scope than those officially assumed by the Church. Christians must accept the various temporal duties related to their state of life. Like all citizens, they must take to heart all human values entrusted by God not to the Church but to their consciences as men and as Christians. And they must do so in a special way in the light of their faith. They must devote themselves to these labors with all their might not only because of the religious repercussions they may expect from them, but also without dividing their lives into watertight compartments that would impair their sense of balance and their apostolic effectiveness.

Thus the Christian physician will take a real interest in the health of his patients because of the respect his faith demands for all divine works. Health is a tool in man's ascent to God, and hence has objective value independently of the use the cured patient may make of it. Whether a patient is a believer or not, a saint or a sinner, his health is worth the trouble the physician will take to restore it. It may happen that health regained will merely prolong the patient's capacity to sin. But that is an eventuality that does not concern the physician as such. Christian faith commits him to the most effective practice of medicine. There is no danger of conflict between his professional conscience and his conscience as a Christian. One will merely interpret the other. And even though, as a doctor, it is no concern of his what the patient does with his restored health, he cannot be indifferent to this matter, as a Christian. The Christian doctor, therefore, will do everything he would if he did not have faith. But as a believer, he will be anxious to give his neighbor everything that

Christian charity can give to those who are in spiritual as well as physical distress.

It will be the same for the big industrialist and the factory worker. They will have at heart the temporal values to which they devote their efforts. They will be very much interested in the technological progress placed in their hands, and rejoice to be able to offer their fellows means of being more completely men. As Christians they will also hope that the material well-being whose artisans they are may contribute to spiritual growth.

Believers and unbelievers can therefore work in complete harmony and with equal energy for the cause of human progress. The faith of the believers will give them a deep interest in all their human tasks. Knowing that nature comes from God and must return to Him, they will be receptive to opportunities for human progress as well as to the inspirations of grace.

Difficulties in making practical judgments and their diversity

The Christian can and must respect purely natural values, have high regard for the unbeliever's efforts, and even collaborate in them. However, it would seem the Christian is under obligation to commit himself in practice to these efforts only in the limited measure compatible with the austere commandment of resignation taught in the Gospel.

For the Christian is in constant danger of forgetting God and thinking only of God's work; of substituting a life of generosity for an authentic life of faith; of depending on natural means of moral elevation more than on prayer and humble trust in the Almighty; of losing sight not only of his dependence as a creature, but also of his original disgrace and repeated sins; of ensconcing himself in the present life and ceasing to hope sincerely for the life to come.

While he must see objective value in temporal progress, he must remember that it is a value that is temporary and conditional. In the event that those who benefit from this progress do not ultimately find God, then all the labor devoted to progress will in fact have been wasted. Must not the Christian, then, take part in the human effort toward progress with fear and trembling lest he do his fellow men a disservice instead of helping them? Does not his baptism require him to think and act like a citizen of another world?

Perhaps we should be more specific and, without denying the objective dignity of natural values, say that the believer must, for imperious psychological reasons, beware of any activity that might tend to dull his supernatural sense and lead him to substitute the accidental for the essential both in his personal life and in his efforts to cooperate with others.

If believers and unbelievers are to join forces, obviously they must first of all agree on the hierarchy of values that are to guide the development of man in accordance with his nature. The Church can encourage only supernaturally inspired humanism.

Acceptance of supernaturally inspired humanism implies acceptance of the principle of mortification. Renouncement is necessary in each of our activities, if they are to be truly human. Even our most praiseworthy affections become degrading if they engross us to the exclusion of everything else. Loyalty to family or to country, to justice or to culture becomes monstrous when it is intolerant, when it leaves no room for other forms of generosity. Even mother love cannot go uncurbed, but must sometimes be ready to yield to other loves. [1] To set up any of this earth's goods as an absolute is to pervert it and to pervert ourselves. It is to go headlong toward psychological unbalance or moral degradation.

We must practice renouncement in all things in order to maintain our equilibrium in all things. We need renouncement not only because of the objective gradation of the many goods that we must seek with a respect for right order, but also because of our own lack of self-mastery. In order to give each thing no more than its rightful place, we need a margin of safety. The relativity of everything that attracts us demands detachment on our part, to help us maintain effective control over all our appetites.

This natural law of mortification finds support in Revelation. Divine teaching on our condition as redeemed sinners throws

---

[1] We have already broached this idea when discussing the necessity of subordinating the good of the individual to the good of the whole community required for authentic human progress.

considerable light on the conclusions to be drawn from reflection on what we are. The Church has condemned the illuminati who taught unrestrained yielding to instinct, and also the sages who were overly confident in man's natural goodness. In so doing she has been faithful to the teachings of her Founder, as exemplified in His words and example, on returning to God by the way of the Cross. The rigorous demands of the supernatural order agree with those we learn through our observation of concrete realities.

And while the supernatural order is in accord with the natural order, its demands go much further. In fact Revelation tells us that in the supernatural order death is the path of access to life, suffering is the leaven of joy, trials pave the road to beatitude. It teaches us that defeat—the defeat of Calvary and all those that continue it—possesses an efficacy in God's eyes incommensurable with the results achieved through human means. It introduces us into the world of invisible realities where the present fades into insignificance before the future offered to our hope. For in that invisible world the profound values we already possess by anticipation make us realize that earthly successes are often only false appearances. But this teaching gives the world new dimensions, without destroying what reason tells us of it. It does not imply hostility to human progress, but calls upon us to joyfully accept deprivation of this progress, and even to prefer such deprivation, out of respect for the total reality that only Revelation can intimate to us.

Christ went straight to essentials when He stressed the limitations of human wisdom, and taught us the importance of renouncement even with regard to things we have legitimate reasons to desire. If we walk in His light, we shall accept all our responsibilities as men; whereas if we are chiefly concerned with obeying the dictates of reason we run the risk of being too reasonable to understand anything about the audacities of love. Those who do not have faith and obey only their reason are in danger of betraying reason by their rationalism. For example, in trying to make wise provision for the future, we are in danger of becoming avaricious. Purely human virtues can easily become vices in the man who has a weak faith or no faith at all, for his first loyalty is to his own ego.

The only way we can break out of our egocentricity and surrender to God is through a spontaneous self-offering. A man cannot be compelled to have faith, nor can he be compelled to go beyond reason in the free renouncement of legitimate aspirations. Therefore the Christian cannot demand renouncement of those who do not share his belief, or even compel his brothers in the faith to accept it by force. While he can and must be the apostle of the Gospel, he has no right to disclaim any interest in the improvement of man's temporal lot simply because the beneficiary will not use his advantages to reach up to God. Obviously, a Christian may not remain indifferent to the progress of faith, but he must also lend his support to efforts to make the world a better place on the human level.

A civilization can retain its equilibrium only if the progress of men's hearts keeps pace with material progress. There will be disharmony if it tries to solve its technological problems solely by moral uplift, but the unbalance will usually go much deeper if concern for material things leads to disregard for the things of the spirit. If material progress is to remain human, it must be accompanied by a strengthening of spiritual influences. It is true that the practice of charity cannot take the place of economic and social growth; but it is a far greater evil for economic and social rationalization to culminate in a soulless society.

Technological advances make possible a more perfect liberation of man's higher faculties, even though they make greater demands on his intellect. The development of man's natural capacities can contribute to the deepening of his religious life, even though it sometimes makes the practice of his religion more difficult. The more complex the balance between divergent forces, the more delicate it becomes. Education lays one open to aberrations of thought to which the illiterate are immune. Refinement of soul increases man's capacity for suffering and makes him more vulnerable. The life of a priest demands greater vigilance than that of a layman. The contemplative's spiritual health requires more safeguards than that of the man of action. It is the counsel of laziness to oppose material progress because it demands greater effort in training man's higher faculties. Likewise, to discourage the development of man's natural talents because it would call for additional effort to develop his religious life to the same level, amounts to defrauding God.

A certain aspect of civilization may be objectively good in itself as well as in its relation to the whole. And it may none the less be undesirable because of accidental circumstances. Man's progress can be a threat to his religious life. He may come to realize that in practice his religion suffers from certain deficiencies because it is human as well as divine. In such a situation, Christians are justified in turning away from human concerns and devoting their efforts to achieving the religious progress necessary to make the best use of human values. While these efforts may prove to be awkward and not entirely successful, this should be no reason for incriminating Christianity as such or for considering belief in eternal life as a threat to humanism.

In a rapidly developing world, the Church's work becomes more demanding but her successes are also more perfect. To the extent that the present-day factory worker is more of a man than the slave of earlier times—and granted he is equal in charity—he is better fitted to be what God expects of him. And so as civilization advances the Church cannot refuse to take on more delicate tasks by virtue of her obligation to encourage man's development as man.

The diversity of vocations

There is an analogy between the demands of religion on a progressing world, and the demands for man's spiritual ascent amid material progress. In both instances, men are called upon to devote themselves more exclusively to the triumph of moral values. If civilization is to remain on an even keel, it needs men who are professionally dedicated to the life of the spirit. And if Christianity is to thrive in such a civilization, it must have men who are professionals of evangelical perfection. The Church cannot be reproached for encouraging societies of men and women who practice renouncement of the world in the highest degree, who refuse the easy life, take no part in technological advances, and give only a subordinate place even to art and culture. One of their social uses is to be witnesses to God on this earth.

Now the religious is not indifferent to the world; he did not retire to a cloister out of contempt for his brothers. He knows that only God deserves the loyalty of his whole being and abandonment of everything else. He also knows that search for God gives value to everything else, and that a Christian life spent in the performance of temporal duties is a life full of meaning before God and rich in merit.

The Church is constantly reminding her children of the evangelical counsels, and teaching the intrinsic superiority of the religious state over life in the world. And yet she knows all states of life are needed to make a world. The mystics who have written the sternest pages on the nothingness of created things and on the radical self-stripping necessary for the pursuit of perfection, also know this. The Gospel, the Church, and the saints are unanimous in asking all men, in all conditions of life, not to scorn anything that God has created, but also not to become enslaved to any attachment that might be merely an expression of the instinct for pleasure.

The only form of attachment categorically forbidden to the Christian is attachment to self, egoism. The more noble a love, the more it increases our capacity to love. An elevating love does not monopolize the soul, but enables it to extend its love to many. So it is when we love God. This love does not imprison the heart, but makes it freer. Attachment to God does not destroy other affections, but transforms them. All members of Christian society must have one thing in common—whether they are laborers or successful businessmen, men of action or men of science, mothers of many children or virgins consecrated to God—and that is freedom from egoism. Christian life in the world is a life of commitment as well as of self-forgetfulness. Each one must give a place to material goods and spiritual riches, according to his own circumstances and the extent that freedom of soul demands it. The choice of a particular state of life or of a particular attitude within that state does not consist in establishing a proper balance between concessions to egoism and the practice of detachment, but in living a life of the greatest possible effective charity and the least egoism.

Every life needs work and rest. Rest must not be a concession to sloth, but a means of working better. Hours of tense effort must be balanced with moments of relaxation. And yet pleasure should not be sought as a means of satisfying our sensuality, but as a help to maintaining our balance and ability for self-giving. The decision to seek pleasure on the part of the Christian implies, unconsciously perhaps but no less deeply, an obligation and a promise of effort. The same criterion applies to choosing a way of life and all one's activities. These choices must be governed by the intention to serve God as perfectly as possible, in accordance with the aptitudes He has given each one of us and the circumstances in which He has placed us: never by a shrewd calculation of the portion to be given to God and to our instincts. Only then can the Christian dedicate himself to temporal tasks within the limits prescribed by religion. This does not mean that all his interests must be religious in character.

The Gospel and the Church are realistic. They impose the same law on all, but require different applications of it according to the condition of each one. The Christian spirit of sacrifice is demanded of the man of wealth and the religious alike. But since temperament, past experience, aptitudes and obligations differ, each one will have to find his own way of safeguarding his freedom of soul. None of us can practice renouncement in general; each of us must choose the renouncement best adapted to his state of life.

True, the religious state is intrinsically more perfect than life in the world. And yet the conscious choice of secular activities on the part of the Christian does not mean capitulation, resignation to his weakness or to circumstances, but rather the generous acceptance of God in all the concrete realities that express His Will. The bishop's state of life is more perfect than that of the simple priest, and yet no one reproaches a priest for not brooding over the fact that he is not called to the episcopate. The Church does not call all priests to be bishops, nor does she call all the faithful to enter the religious life. What she asks of each one is to be where God wants him to be, and in the manner God wants.

Of all the Christian denominations, the Catholic Church makes the greatest demands. In her religious houses she officially organized with the greatest solicitude and austerity a life according to the evangelical counsels; and she alone requires celibacy of her clergy. And at the same time she is the religion most receptive to every aspect of human life, the most humanistic of the religions. If she accepted as members only the faithful determined to leave the life of the world, she would obviously deprive herself of the many ways of understanding Christ's message implicit in the various states of life. Manual laborers have a more spontaneous and deeper grasp of certain aspects of Christian doctrine than do intellectuals; Christians committed to the obligations of a family and a profession have a more concrete and sometimes a more exacting grasp than do religious of certain aspects of the Gospel. There is also a way of pleading God's cause that belongs to life in the world. In apostolic action as in efforts at personal conversion, the Church does not propose the same task to everyone. She asks each one to be where God expects him to be, and in the manner God expects of him.

No Christian can deliberately limit himself to doing what is obligatory, while excluding explicitly and in principle the pursuit of greater perfection. And yet the more perfect may not be desirable in particular cases. Each one must take to heart the role assigned to him, without forgetting the total context of Christian living, and also without growing discouraged at the limits to which his role restricts him.

Each Christian must discern his own path and practice the form of renunciation most effective for his particular vocation. He must distinguish in his own life between what is obligatory and what is optional. He must make his decision honestly, courageously, and persevere in it with fervor. And this he can do only in the light of the Gospel and with the help of grace.

He will succeed only if the Church helps him. And so the Church must remind him, according to circumstances, of the value and urgency of temporal tasks, or of their ultimate end which is rooted in the supernatural life. She must also on occasion remind him of the hold sin has on the world and of the need to emancipate himself from it by renunciation. When she sees God's work jeopardized by a false spiritualism, she will defend the material universe and the natural virtues. Alarmed by the stresses and strains in temporal society, she will insist on the urgent need of social action or on the conditions for peace among peoples. Faced with the upsurge of materialism that scorns the life of sacrifice and the spirit of renouncement, she will remind Christians of the reality of sin and the Redemption by the Cross.

These various reminders are all necessary, and in every age it has been difficult to be faithful to the constellation of truths she teaches. We are constantly in danger of forgetting the demands of Christian commitment to temporal things and stressing only the obligations of the life of faith. We are likewise inclined to forget that the solution of temporal problems, in itself, remains outside the religious domain; and even if social progress helps to make better Christians, those who have deserted the Church will return to her only if they take an interest not only in social problems but above all in the Christian life and in the spirit of detachment that is its law.

A glance at history

We have been arguing from dogmatic principles. Now let us turn to the facts, and cast a rapid glance at the history of the Church.

First, let us open the Gospel. There the Lord denounces all self-seeking. He puts us on our guard against attachments that paralyze us even though they sometimes give us the illusion of liberty. He teaches poverty of spirit much more than the spirit of work, prudence, and the other solid virtues of human wisdom. He praises poverty and suffering. But in dealing with the sick, He did more than give them lessons on the spiritual profit to be gained from their pain. He distributed bread to a hungry crowd that had followed Him; He refilled His friends' supply of wine at the wedding feast. He gave us the good Samaritan as a model, a man who was concerned not only with the spiritual welfare of his neighbor, but who made use of all the medical knowledge available at that time to help restore him to health. The Master does not tell us that it would have been better to teach the wounded victim the purifying value of suffering. On the contrary, He gave the Samaritan high praise for having taken time from his own occupations and used every human means to improve the unfortunate man's temporal lot.

The first disciples followed their Master's example. St. Peter, after apologizing for not having any money, restored the paralytic's body to health. St. Paul devoted much effort to collecting funds to relieve the misery of the Christians of Jerusalem.

When the new religion had spread far and wide, there was much discussion on the attitude to take toward Greco-Roman culture and morals. While some writers preached non-participation in this culture, the " humanists " won the day. Tertullian boasted that the Christians did not sulk at the world but on the contrary played an active role in all sectors of the economic and social life of his time.

The Church has never ceased promoting and organizing ways of relieving material want. In the Middle Ages she did not merely provide for the distribution of alms, she went so far as to provide education in agricultural techniques, and took charge of many projects for the common good.

She has always protected the arts, and taken part in all intellectual activities. In our own day, instead of using all her human and other resources in the apostolic ministry, she continues to encourage culture and scientific research, assigning priests and religious to these secular tasks.

Although the Church has not always shown the same interest in human problems in every epoch, and her present concern with the great modern social problems was born in great part from the religious crisis created by the suffering of the proletariat, it is clear that she does not limit her interest to the spiritual needs of man.

At the same time, throughout her history she has encouraged and offered as models saints who have preached and practiced, to the point of heroism, retirement from the world, contempt for the body, and even indifference to culture.

Is there not an inconsistency here?

Admittedly the Church has had her weaknesses in every age. No historian would deny it. But she countenances so many ways of understanding and practicing the ideal of the Gospel because she knows that God's teaching infinitely exceeds what any one historical epoch, man, or system can absorb. She knows that she will never stop discovering new facets of the treasures entrusted to her, or improving her grasp of their many potentialities. There is not and never will be a single, definitive type of Christianity that subsequent ages will merely need to imitate. Christianity is much too rich to be consummated in a single epoch. The Church lives in time, and at every moment of history she discovers and actualizes certain portions of God's plan, more or less perfectly, depending on the potentialities or deficiencies of the moment.

Conclusions

The infallible teaching of the Church has been given detailed expression through the centuries. Without contradicting itself, it has stressed the truths that needed to be safeguarded at particular times. The deposit of faith has been the object of commentaries by the hierarchy, theologians, saints, as well as ordinary Christians who have thought out their religion or understood it by living it. Infallible teaching is limited to essential truths. These are interpreted by non-infallible teachings and Christian thought in an effort to integrate them into world views explaining the problems of various epochs. The same patrimony includes works as diverse as the theology of St. Augustine and that of St. Thomas, and organizations as different as that of the feudal Church and the Church of today.

The matters we have been discussing go far beyond the limits proposed by the infallible teaching of the Church, and would not have been approved by authorized Christian thinkers of every era. St. Augustine, for example, would not readily have admitted the Christian's right to take an interest in science for its own sake, without a religious purpose, or the Church's view that the state has complete autonomy in its own sphere. St. Augustine belonged to his own time, and reflected on the cultural conditions of his epoch. Since that time the Christian community has continued to live and to think. It has made great strides in assessing and interpreting its faith.

St. Thomas had a better insight into the value of purely natural activities, and the relative autonomy that is rightfully theirs. The evolution of culture and of the relations between

Church and State inspired his disciples to carry his thought further. If generally accepted positions today are no longer what they were in antiquity or in the Middle Ages, that is no reason to reproach Christian thought for having developed. To do so would be proof of a most pitiable lack of historic sense. We cannot condemn St. Augustine or the medieval thinkers for not having known our problems.

The doctrine we are presenting leaves room for very divergent positions on the practical orientation Christianity should be given today. Some will insist on the need to rediscover everything that the primacy of God and renouncement of the world should mean for sinners redeemed by the Cross. Others will stress the duty of Christians to commit themselves resolutely to the solution of temporal problems and to promote solutions conformable to evangelical principles as well as natural law. Both of these approaches have something to teach us.

Like the Christians of every epoch, we must work, reflect, and pray so that, with intransigent respect for the deposit of faith, with filial loyalty to the directives of the Church, with love for her entire spiritual heritage, and vigilant attention to the problems of our own time, we may be docile to the inspirations of grace and write the new page in the history of Christianity that God expects of us. This page will contain the same dogma, moral teaching, spiritual and apostolic ideals as the earlier pages, but they will be assimilated and put into practice in a way heretofore unknown, because never before has God given the Church the century in which we live. God asks our contemporaries, as He did our ancestors, to constantly renew the harmony between eternal principles and the changing world. To strive to achieve this harmony is certainly not opportunism. It is obedience to these principles.

VI   Death and life in Christ

Living as " risen men "

As baptized Christians, united to Christ in the Mass, we are participants in the paschal mystery. Our Christian conviction has made us die permanently to ourselves and become sharers in the life of the Lord Jesus.

As members of the risen Christ, we must live as risen men, i.e., supernaturally. We must not act in accordance with nature, and yet we must act. We must want not our own will but the Will of the God who causes us to die and to live. We must want His Will to be done in us, rather than choose our own goal in life and claim we can attain it through our own efforts. We must really want God's Will. To live by Christ and to want Him to live more fully in us is to strive toward an active passivity. It is a matter of letting God have His way with us, while we remain docile and totally at His service. And that does not mean remaining inert! To practice " holy indifference " does not mean being indifferent. It means renouncing anxiety, while dreading quietism; it means trying to live the life of heaven, with a healthy fear of falling into angelism.

We must be at once idealists and realists, mystics and pragmatists, men of prayer and organizers. We must put our trust in supernatural means, and doggedly use all available earthly means. We must live in a spirit of prayer, and yet fear lest prayer be only or above all a form of evasion.

We must seek God alone, and yet be deeply interested in men; work out of love of God, and yet also with gusto.

We must be dead and yet alive, committed and yet free, interested and yet detached, taking everything to heart and yet clinging to nothing. Unless we succeed in living by this paradoxical attitude, our Christianity will lack authenticity. Either we shall be outside the current of the supernatural life or outside the demanding and prosaic realities of our everyday life. We must live and preach this kind of Christianity, if we do not want to propagate a sweet pietism or moralism that will not bring us to authentic conversion.

But is not such a program a mirage or a mellifluous flow of meaningless words?

Prayer of abandonment

To give us light in this important matter, let us reread the decisive prayer composed by the great French Jesuit, Father Leonce de Grandmaison.

November 1. Fifth meditation. The Three Classes.

I am attaching herewith, on a separate sheet, my self-offering to God made during this meditation. I am under the winepress. No prayer ever cost me so dearly, since I made my decision to enter the Society fifteen years ago, as I walked among the Portuguese laurels. Each word of this offering, which had been forced upon me and which I made with a bitterness that did not exclude peace, tore my heart out. It seemed as if a red iron was branding me each time, to purify me, to burn away the human alloy of my affections, tastes, and desires. I saw clearly that I was incapable of this sacrifice by myself, and I was not conscious of the love of the One who dictated it. The most I could do was submit, say *Amen*, close my eyes, and abandon myself—not like a well-loved son, but as a servant, a repenter, a penitent, with bared back, feeling the blows, sustained by the strength of grace and yet not feeling its action, acting through pure faith, against all human reason. That entire evening, I remained under the impact of it, submissive and bleeding.

November 2. Here is the prayer I said last night:

I arrived in my room for the five o'clock exercise,
firmly resolved to refuse God nothing, but to offer Him
everything without reservation, and I kept thinking of the
words of General de Sonis: " In returning to the Army, I
am condemning myself to death.   God will have mercy on
me if He so wills... etc. "   And I foresaw that I would
have to wage a fierce battle: indeed, I do not think I have
made a more painful offering since I entered the Society.
I felt as if I were under the winepress, especially as I was
saying this prayer because I had to do it, without any natural
or supernatural attraction on my part, but on the contrary
with horror, realizing that, naturally speaking, it was
fantastic and unreasonable.   Roughly, here is the burden
of the offering:

My God, I accept from Your hand this life of perfection, of total self-stripping, of extreme purity, which the
devil holds up to me as a death; and which is a death, in a
very real sense.   I accept, therefore, to live henceforth only
for You, to live a pure life, renouncing (insofar as it depends
on me) the natural pleasure of all affection, of intellectual
influence and the influence of friendship; I accept the partial
or total sacrifice, when and as You choose, of my every
aptitude and talent for letters, philosophy, theology, history,
teaching and spiritual direction.   I likewise accept the
affective and effective sacrifice of all my present or future
friendships, of all my artistic or intellectual tastes.   In other
words, I accept (if it be Your good pleasure) to live with
mediocre people, far from those who are dear to me, surrounded by ugly and commonplace things, exercising meager
influence on a few vulgar persons, and often being changed
about.   Moreover, I agree not to seek rest and pleasure in
any earthly thing, in any joy, in any created beauty, and to
see my life covered with these ashes that extinguish all
human satisfaction.   And therefore I agree to renounce my
family and the joys of keeping close to its members in mind
and heart; to renounce my friends, to the point of becoming
for even the closest of them as if I no longer existed on earth,
and to act in all things (insofar as my feelings are concerned)
as if they no longer existed for me.   Thus I pledge myself
to serve You with perfect purity of intention, amid trials,
misfortunes, in old age or sickness, without any human

support except from superiors, doing menial tasks, forgotten and neglected even by those who have esteemed me or been my friends. And I accept all this, so that I may serve You with purity of intention and for Your greater glory, not because I am heartless, but because I believe and I know that You can compensate, and return a hundredfold to those whom it is my obligation to love and whom I do love, the little I myself would do for them.

I accept this life without consolation or visitation of Your special grace, but, as I do this evening, under constraint and duress, impelled not by the attraction of love but by naked duty, and solely out of the desire to do Your Will. I accept to be treated not as a son, but as a servant, not as a friend but as a repentant sinner ready to be beaten. I bare my back, hard as this may seem to me. *Hic ure, hic seca...* *in flagella paratus sum.*

I accept this life of sacrifice, even though it seems impossible to me, absolutely beyond my strength, above and almost against nature. I accept it with naked and pure faith, deeming that if You make demands You will give strength proportioned to Your demands, and not consolations but the courage to persevere to the end.

I want to be happy in this life, for I consider it above my merits.

And thus I abandon myself to You, my God and Lord Jesus, through the hands of Your Mother, beseeching Your love and Your grace, and no other reward but You.

November 1, 1900. [1]

What did Father de Grandmaison do immediately after making this offering to God? He devoted himself to literature, philosophy, theology, history, teaching, and spiritual direction. He did not break off with his friends or his family. He did not bury his artistic or intellectual tastes, he accepted consolations joyfully. Does this mean he was unfaithful to the oblation of his long retreat? On the contrary, his life incontestably possessed a beautiful supernatural unity. To convince ourselves of this we need only read his biography or his spiritual writings. A much simpler procedure, would be to compare the two photo-

[1] Jules LEBRETON, S. J., *Le Père Léonce de Grandmaison*, 2nd edition (Paris, 1932), pp. 126-128.

graphs used as illustrations in Father Lebreton's biography of
him: the portrait of the young Jesuit with the willful face, who
knew what he wanted (perhaps a little too well), and the peaceful
face of the old religious, emptied of himself and abandoned to God.

What, then, is the significance of the text we have just read?

Docility to the Spirit

First of all, let us note that we are confronted here not merely
with a " retreat resolution, " made with stoic dispositions. We
are in the presence of a prayer: the soul is holding a dialogue
with God, and its attitude before Him is truly one of " active
passivity. " Let us go over some of the retreatant's words:
" Each word of this offering, forced upon me... The most I
could do was submit, say *Amen*, close my eyes, and abandon
myself... acting through pure faith... My God, I accept... I
abandon myself to You. "

This is no mere decision to amend one's ways, inspired by
good will. The initiative has come from outside, and the
retreatant simply accepts it. It is not an act of spiritual muscle-
flexing, with a view to mobilizing all the resources of one's being
to attain self-mastery and exceed one's natural capacities. It
is an act of abandonment, of self-surrender. It is an episode
in a life of surrender to God, and not in a man's effort to perfect
himself. These lines belong to the climate of thought of Father
de Grandmaison's *Écrits spirituels*, [2] which lay so much stress on
docility to the Holy Spirit. The offering we have just quoted
is an act of submission to grace, to an austere grace, thriving on
aridity, " with a bitterness that does not exclude peace. "

Besides, Father de Grandmaison made this act of docility
only after having made this petition: " O Lord... inspire me with
the supernatural discernement I need. " In the light of this
inspiration, he realized it was absolutely impossible for him to
refuse or to pick and choose. He made his great offering " because
he had to do it. " It had been " dictated " [3] to him.

---

[2] These writings have been published in English under the following
titles: *We and the Holy Spirit; Come, Holy Spirit; Tongues of Fire;* and *Send
Forth Thy Spirit*, by Fides Publishers (Notre Dame, Indiana).

[3] J. LEBRETON, *op. cit.*, p. 126.

An act of love

This self-surrender to God, made without any feeling of attraction for it, was really an act of love. It had its roots in reflection on what God has a right to expect from us, not on the obstacles to be overcome in order to achieve perfect self-mastery. Its goal was not to attain greatness of soul, strength, or balance, but to belong to God solely out of a desire to do His Will. He was seeking God Himself, not His gifts. " I abandon myself to You, my God and Lord Jesus, through the hands of Your Mother, beseeching Your love and Your grace, and no other reward but You. "

Prayer

The retreatant was not determined to make a success of his life, to become " somebody. " He was inspired not by ambition, but solely by the desire to make room within himself for the God of love and holiness. He wanted " to refuse Him nothing. " Pride was not his motive. It was not for the pleasure of persecuting himself that he was so hard on himself. He did not condemn himself to death out of a delight in death. Let no one insinuate that he had a morbid, masochistic attraction for suffering! Christianity, which finds typical expression in Léonce de Grandmaison's offering, condemns direct suicide, while demanding indirect suicide. To love God is to consent to die.

This is true of every love. People don't usually get married out of a desire for mortification, but anyone who gets married without realizing he or she is committing himself to a life of mortification is sadly mistaken. Marriage, like all love, is one of the ways by which God makes us accept a death to self that we have not willed directly but accept goodnaturedly almost without thinking about it, as all our attention is focussed on the love that fills our heart. Men without number have become courageous and devoted husbands, even without realizing it, under the impulsion of a great love. And these same men would have become selfish, moody, and lazy, had they remained bachelors. To agree to take a wife is to renounce one form of tranquility in exchange for peace of another sort. Likewise, to agree to bring children into the world means renouncing the peace of lovers' tête-à-têtes. But when conjugal love is sacrificed in

this way, it relives with a new flame in the love of fatherhood and
motherhood.   To be willing to have more children is to sacrifice
those one already has.   And yet when children have brothers
and sisters, they are not loved less but in a different way.   To
accept to take an interest in the children of others, in addition
to one's own, is to mortify the exclusive love one might have for
one's own flesh and blood; but love of one's own family is thereby
transfigured.

Every love involves both death and resurrection.   Every love
makes us die and live again.   And this is incomparably truer of
love of God than of any other.   Father de Grandmaison was
motivated by love of God.   He wrote the offering we have
quoted not because his intellect was fired by an idea but because
his heart was in love with Someone.

We are not speaking here of an emotional attachment, but of
God's total possession of a personality.   We are speaking not
merely of the awakening of sentiment, or even of the naked will,
but of surrender, to God, of one's entire being.

Father de Grandmaison's prayer came from his " heart, "
thus understood, and not from his emotions.   In fact, far from
being dominant, his emotions rebelled against his action.   He
explained that he was " impelled not by the attraction of love,
but by naked duty, and solely out of the desire to do Your Will. "
He described himself as being " without any natural or supernatural   attraction. "   Obviously,   the   supernatural   attraction
existed, but without the usual external appearances.   That is what
he meant when he affirmed that he offered himself " with horror. "
He was also aware of committing himself to something " unreasonable. "   And yet he could not have been more reasonable.
Thus, a marriage of love is not a marriage of convenience, and yet
the folly it may involve can and must be reasonable.   When we
pass from the habitual level of mental activity to a deeper level, we
come to attractions and prudential judgments that deserve to be
called reasonable, even though they are very different from the
attractions and prudences on the surface of the mind.

Thus, the object of his desire to give himself, rising from the
deepest recesses of his being, was not an abstract ideal.   It was
the will of the personal God to whom he had dedicated himself.
This was truly love in the sense we are giving it, for it wa

essentially the meeting of two living beings, two persons, and thus differed from fidelity to a principle or to a law.

Only love enables us to will mortification in a way that is not morbid. If sacrifice were the goal instead of simply a means of loving, if death to self were not at the service of love, all this renouncement would be indefensible. It would seem " naturally speaking, fantastic and unreasonable... above and almost against nature. " It would be quite patently against nature if it were not the expression of a love, which itself is a response to love. And of the response as well as the invitation, God Himself is the source. It is His heart that inspires man's heart to sacrifice.

Father de Grandmaison did not consent to this renouncement with an individualistic view of his relationship to God. He was concerned with God's love for others as well as for himself. He also felt responsibility for what the Lord might expect from his apostolate for the good of others. He felt himself called to make this sacrifice so that he might be at his neighbor's service with greater purity of intention, and not only so that he himself might belong more completely to God.

Only consecration to a superior love makes it possible to renounce love without becoming hard. The goal of Christian mortification of the affections is not to stop loving, but to have greater love for God and for those among whom He places us. Such a consecration does not lead to isolation. Through it we lovingly entrust to God those who are dear to us, wishing for them a good that God alone can give. We are simply means of helping them to attain that good, and means that can be done without. Thus is purified a desire to influence others that might be too earthly and mingled with self-seeking, too easily sullied with feverish intervention or at least with a lack of humility and discretion. " And I accept all this, so that I may serve You with purity of intention and for Your greater glory, not because I am heartless, but because I believe and I know that You can compensate, and return a hundredfold to those whom it is my obligation to love and whom I do love, the little I myself would do for them. "

This profound attitude, which places the whole man under the impulsion of the spirit of faith, is not hatred of self or absence of love for others. It is a supernatural love of God, of others, and of self. It is charity, the echo of divine love in the retreatant's soul, the work of the Holy Spirit who implants words in our souls that do not come from us.

The relationship between God and the soul He is guiding is a mystery of love, but it is also a mystery of mercy. Father de Grandmaison plunged with blind trust into what seemed a dark night. But like St. Paul, he knew in whom he had placed his confidence, and he realized he was not worthy of His love. He refused to make any demands, but simply offered himself. He did not forget that divine love cannot be a superficial show of affection, but must make austere demands on the sinner whom it seeks to liberate. He acknowledged that he had received from the Redemption whatever he might be worth in God's eyes, and he wanted to approach God as a redeemed man. He agreed in advance to anything God would ask of the repentant sinner that he was. He did not approach the Most High brazenly. He was too deeply aware of who the God of holiness is, and what he was himself. In his authentically supernatural attitude, he included the supernatural spirit of penance: " I accept to be treated not as a son, but as a servant, not as a friend but as a repentant sinner ready to be beaten. " These are words that the Gospel places on the lips of the prodigal son.

To see oneself as a sinner, even though one knows one has been redeemed, leads not to despair but to hope. The man who has attained a better understanding of God and of his own misery is capable of undertaking the impossible peacefully, even joyously: " I accept this life of sacrifice, even though it seems impossible to me, absolutely beyond my strength, above and almost against nature.... I want to be happy in this life, for I consider it above my merits. "

Response to a love: knowing the Father's heart

Only the spirit of faith can impel anyone to undertake such a venture, one that is humanly impossible. Only love of God —a love nourished in the sinner's heart by the remembrance of God's forgiveness—can make possible the uncompromising perseverance that will be a fulfillment and not a mutilation. But since this love can only be God's work in man, we must, if we would dare aspire to it, be sure of the Father's love, a love that puts a little of His heart into the heart of His creature. The retreatant's prayer, completely founded on faith, and unsupported by emotion, was admirable for its boldness and trust. Father de Grandmaison realized he was making an appalling sacrifice. He consented to it because he believed in it. " I accept it with naked and pure faith, deeming that if You make demands You will give strength proportioned to Your demands. " And he concluded with the simple words: " I abandon myself to You. "

Such was the magnificent courage of a man who dared to believe in love, who dared to take God's call seriously and to rely on His grace. Father de Grandmaison did not rely on himself, as he repeated over and over, and this was the source of his strength. The reason he did not pull back, or disfigure his vocation and blind himself to its demands, the reason he did not reduce the task to small sacrifices whittled down to his size, was because he reacted not merely as a generous man, but as a believer.

Father de Grandmaison did not know where God was leading him, what anguish he would have to accept in the path he was entering, or what defeats he would suffer in the pursuit of this impossible heroism. But he had only one desire: " the desire to do Your Will. " He put his trust in this Will with a peace stripped of all consolation, but an authentic peace nevertheless. In the depths of this theological life, he had surrendered himself into God's hands with complete serenity. He dared to think quite calmly that God loved him enough to call him to His friendship even through this purification, that God took such an interest in him as to expect a great deal of him; and that as a consequence, God in His mercy would proportion His grace to His demands. He dared to pray with quiet hope that God's Will be done. For he knew that God's Will is His forgiving love; and he was ready to collaborate, happen what may, with this love that sets on fire and pacifies. Let divine Love act in him without hindrance! Shaken but serene, he knew that he would not be deceived. He made a *tabula rasa* of all his reticences, and herein lay the core of his offering. He would no longer approach the Most High with reservations and conditions. Instead, he said an unconditional

" Yes! " to the work of love that the God of holiness wanted
to accomplish in his heart. For he understood that God loved
him enough to draw him to Himself with powerful arms, and to
want to possess his heart here on earth and for all eternity.

Father de Grandmaison had made contact with the transcendent God, the Incommensurable One, the One who is also
Love and Mercy, who is at once terrible and comforting, transcendent because He is infinite Love, and totally incommensurable
with us because He is ineffably purifying Mercy. When he
recognized his God and his Father, he had the courage not
to avoid His glance, and not to close his ears to His voice. His
answer was a deeply trusting, even if tremulous, *fiat*. His senses
and his reason were in turmoil, but his theological life opened his
soul to the Master's action in a spirit of supernatural peace.

The state of the retreatant, as described by his own words,
was a paroxysm. It was salutary, but it must not be exacerbated.
There was something artificial about it because it was caused by
an overall view of demands that he would be called on to meet
not all at once but in a less tragic way—in the small currency of
countless minor sacrifices. Realizing this, his spiritual director
advised him " to accept all the sacrifices already made or yet to be
made, *in toto*, without going into further details for the moment. " [4]
This tension could not be allowed to last or to become a permanent
source of exasperation. His emotions needed to be quieted, peace
must triumph over fear and gradually imbue all his faculties.

The means of achieving peace

This is precisely what happened during the following days.
Father de Grandmaison inquired into the means available to him
for effectively putting into practice a consecration as all-embracing
as his. He was serene. He decided to make what he called
" an election of confidence. "

First of all, he placed himself again in God's presence.

Whereas, in the light of God where I try to remain,
God is He who is and I am he who is not, and therefore,

[4] J. LEBRETON , *op. cit.*, p. 127, note 1.

being a creature that comes totally from God, I must be totally His; whereas, having been gratuitously raised to divine sonship and to the blessed privileges that follow from it, I must belong to God as a loyal son jealous of His Father's honor and eager to resemble Him; whereas, having been redeemed by our Lord Jesus Christ who was delivered up for me, I must belong to God as one snatched from eternal death at the price of the freely shed blood of my innocent elder Brother; whereas, being a sinner, I have used God's graces against Him and therefore, since I am unfaithful and adulterous, I must belong to God as a repenter, forgiven out of pure goodness and ready for the blows he deserves; whereas, notwithstanding my ingratitudes, God has called me to His intimate friendship and to share the life and work of His beloved Son by making me a religious, a priest, and a Jesuit, and I must therefore belong to God as a disciple of our Lord.... [5]

In the light of God's merciful love, the retreatant took a good look at himself: first at what is common to all men in his condition, then at what experience had taught him of his own needs. He then turned to practical resolutions.

Whereas, until now I have been impeded in the pure service of God by a certain pusillanimity that made me dread grace and doubt its efficacy, and above all by undue attachment to my natural and earthly happiness, an attachment that led me, in fact and in desire, to seek rest and pleasure in created things, human truths, beauty, and affections too little related to God; whereas, this attitude resulted in a state of habitual sadness at the realization that my heart would never have here on earth the complete rest it desired; and resulted likewise in a passionate attachment to the sciences, letters, and arts, to human esteem and affection, coming between God and me during prayer, feeding my ambition and desire to please men, my self-esteem and satisfaction in human consolations, and arousing an all too natural anxiety lest I lose these pleasures as well as chagrin that I did not have enough of them.

[5] J. LEBRETON, *op. cit.*, p. 129.

Whereas, this attachment to created things is what causes me the greatest concern for my religious future, and could be most instrumental in preventing me from attaining the sanctity my vocation demands and to which I know God has deigned to call me; whereas, also, the probable order of God's Providence will commit me to a life in which I shall have to renounce this attachment in my heart without renouncing the studies, friendships, and loves that gave rise to it; a life in which I shall have to strive for success without really wanting it, dedicate myself with all my strength to works that I love without becoming enslaved by them, to love much without ceasing to love purely—and whereas this is to live in the midst of fire without being burned, to be in the world without being of the world; whereas I am utterly lacking in the strength this demands of me; whereas, nevertheless, my vocation also seems to call me to accept peacefully and even joyously all providential dispositions of my life (health, occupations, setbacks, losses, separations, ingratitudes, failures, dryness, desertions), and whereas, I have even less strength to face these things than I have to work purely for the glory of God:

I resolve to ask God with humility and trust the special grace I need to persevere in this unselfish, joyous, and filial abandonment. Obviously this grace consists in seeing, in every disposition of God in my regard, His very wise and paternal hand upon me,—and to see in my labors and affections the honor and love of the Father, Master, and Supreme Friend, of the only totally satisfying Good, of the One I love. It is He I want for myself, He that I want for everyone else, and in particular for those whom it is my duty to love more than others. If I did not, my labors and affections would be harmful to me and to them. But, providing grace preserves me in this purity of intention, I shall obtain ineffable benefits for myself and for them, benefits that will not pass.

To repeat, I need this grace of joyful abandoment, of loving and courageous unselfishness, as well as the intimate friendship with my Lord and my God which is the source of these graces. Only Jesus Christ can obtain these things for me, and only the Holy Spirit can communicate and safeguard them.

In order to cooperate with this grace, I am resolved to pray, since prayer is the only efficacious means of attaining to this divine friendship.

I shall therefore try—and this is the resolution of my long retreat—to establish more firmly than before this union with God, Father, Son, and Holy Spirit, in the morning during mental prayer made with greater detachment and abandonment of all things to God, and during the Mass that really unites me to God Himself; to renew this union more often, implicitly or explicitly, by a recourse or an elevation of heart to God, either in thought or by a mental and vocal act, a prayer, an aspiration, a word of acquiescence, of professed preference for God, of detachment from created things, by an offering to God of the persons and things I love, so that He may purify my efforts and my affection, by contrition, humility, thanksgiving, or petition.

And may God come to my assistance, through the merits of Jesus Christ, under the protection of the Blessed Virgin and the patronage of SS. Joseph, John, Ignatius, Xavier, and Thomas, of my Guardian Angel and my Patron Saint. [6]

Let us study the plan of this page. The author first casts a glance on the past, and concludes that two things have held him back: first, " a certain pusillanimity that made me dread grace and doubt its efficacy, " and correlatively " undue attachment to my natural and earthly happiness. " Looking to the future, he foresees that this lack of supernatural spirit can turn him away from the sanctity to which God is calling him. He also foresees that, in practice, circumstances will impose a twofold detachment on him. He will have to renounce in spirit activities he really enjoys, and at the same time accept with peace and joy providential conditions of life contrary to his natural aspirations. The path he will have to follow is one of " loving and courageous unselfishness, " of " joyous and filial abandonment. " This is beyond the retreatant's strength, it presupposes " a special grace " to be asked " with humility and trust. " And, he says, this can only be the fruit of " an intimate friendship

[6] J. LEBRETON, *op. cit.*, pp. 129-131.

with my Lord and my God. " His resolution, therefore, must ultimately be to attain to union with God in prayer, on the one hand during privileged moments—notably mental prayer and the Mass—when he will strive to achieve " greater detachment from created things, more respectful trust and filial abandonment of all things to God "; and on the other hand, during the course of each day, when he will renew these dispositions of detachment from created things and attachment to God.

Now these are not just beautiful words. And they were not written in a moment of religious exaltation that would have no morrow. These lines have the sharpness of a diagnosis. The retreatant makes his point, and examines with cold lucidity the concrete applications of his desire to belong to God. He goes from broad, overall views to the practical implications of his loyal adherence to the divine plan, and from beginning to end he strives to be realistic. He has been raised to supernatural sonship. Although he is unworthy of God's graces which he has abused by turning them against Him, he must be " like a disciple of Our Lord. " What does fidelity to this transcendent reality mean in practice in everyday life?

Father de Grandmaison does not choose. Here again, he listens to what is dictated to him. He is satisfied to hear God's call and to interpret the translation of it given him by his temperament, his past, and his work. His tone is always one of docility. He does not try to propose his own plan of holiness. He strives to attain the necessary flexibility to submit to God's plan. He does not know the details of God's plan, but he feels he is asked to ratify it blindly.

His fundamental attitude is one of humble prayer. He surrenders, knowing that this very surrender is more God's action within him than his own, and that perseverance must be the fruit of divine work.

In this text, his agitation and fright seem to have been calmed. The retreatant gives less attention to the harshness of the sacrifice and more to the goodness of God who leads him to it. He sees that he must ask for the grace, on the one hand, to see God's paternal goodness as the origin of everything that happens to him, and, on the other, to look to the Father he loves as the end toward whom all his efforts are directed.

Thus love is the essential reality in all his thinking. The religious must answer the love of the One who deigns to invite him to a life of holiness by silencing all his earthly ambitions and natural desires so that he can devote himself totally to God.

Thinking only of God does not mean forgetting neighbor. It is to love neighbor by wanting him also to possess the one God. " It is He I want for myself, He that I want for everyone else, and in particular for those whom it is my duty to love more than others. But, providing grace preserves me in this purity of intention, I shall obtain ineffable benefits for myself and for them, benefits that will not pass. " As in the prayer of the preceding days, Father de Grandmaison's election is that of a man dedicated to the apostolic life. It is focussed upon the conditions for his own sanctity and for the efficacy of his apostolic action.

We must also consider, in relation to the above quotation, the following words: " Whereas, it is to serve and love, authentically and practically, those whom I have a natural obligation to love and serve, either through gratitude or by providential attraction, to love them with a spiritual and divine affection, free of any alloy of egoism, and destined to endure eternally. " [7] Our Jesuit seems to have a clearer and calmer understanding of what is involved in supernaturalizing his natural affections. Some of the formulas of his earlier prayer were harsh. He spoke of this life of total self-stripping " that the devil holds up to me as a death, and which is a death, " as being " naturally fantastic and unreasonable. " He declared that this radical sacrifice was " above and almost against nature. " He depended on God to compensate those he was sacrificing with himself for the little he could have done for them. Now he sees more clearly that this compensation will not be added on to his renouncement from without, but that the purification of his affections will eliminate only what could have been harmful to his neighbor; and that to love spiritually is to love " authentically and in practice. "

Once he has sincerely accepted from the depths of his heart to be stripped of every affection, he finds himself able to look forward to a life in which he must " love much without ceasing to

---

[7] J. LEBRETON, *op. cit.*, p. 129.

love purely. " He knows that this will not be any easier than if his natural aspirations were in no way satisfied. He is well aware that to want God alone amid labors that he enjoys is beyond his strength. He sees that the indispensable condition for this is " intimate friendship with God. " Finally this interior drama is solved by a clear view of the primordial place prayer must have in his life. He cannot overcome his fear of grace and his attachment to created things except by heart-to-heart contact with God, in which he will renew his " respectful trust " and " filial abandonment, " as well as his " detachment from all created things. " He knows that this friendship with God will also be a gift: " Only Jesus Christ can obtain it for me, only the Holy Spirit can communicate and safeguard it. " Withal, he knows that his soul must be loyally receptive to this gift.

The basic problem, therefore, as Father de Grandmaison sees it, is the authenticity of prayer. His contact with God must be many things at once—" intimate friendship, " " respectful trust, " " filial abandonment, " " detachment from created things, " " offering ... contrition ... gratitude ... petition. " It must be profound and, in a certain sense, continuous. The encounter with God in the morning must be renewed " oftener, implicitly or explicitly. " The great obligation is to live a life of prayer; it is union with God—Father, Son, and Spirit—entered into with the courageous realization of who God is and what man is, whom God calls to a life of divine sonship. This intimacy with God will assure him of the permanent dispositions of joyous abandonment and loving unselfishness that are its natural fruits. Thus only will it be possible for him to achieve something beyond human strength, namely: " To love much without ceasing to love purely, " " to accept peacefully and even joyously all providential dispositions. " Thus will pusillanimity before God be overcome, as well as overly natural attachment to created things. Thus will the spirit of faith and truly supernatural modes of action triumph.

The retreatant now sees himself on a path that will allow him to return to the same tasks as before, while acquitting himself of them in an entirely different spirit. He will be sent back " to studies, friendships, loves, " he will perfect his education, he will teach, he will give spiritual direction. He will do everything he loves to do, but he will see everything in a new light and will accomplish everything with a much deeper sense of self-giving. He will be no less enamored with his work, but his delight in it will be purified of "human alloy." The human element will be present, but transfigured. Everything will have gone through a death and a resurrection, whose source must be constantly sought in God, through prayer.

It will be at once God's work in him and his own work through his receptiveness to grace. It will be a work accomplished in an indissoluble union, God always having the initiative, but the soul never being dispensed of making the personal effort of consenting to it. It will be a life built up in common, in which nothing will be done by man unless God is doing it within him, and in which God will do nothing without calling upon man's active loyalty. Father de Grandmaison does not try to understand this mystery of collaboration between man and God. He is content to believe in it, to know that he can rely on grace, and that if he really does depend on it he will immerse himself in a life of trusting and detached prayer.

And now he is calm, relaxed, boldly ready to take on a superhuman task. As he himself writes:

November 5 (resolutions clarifying the scope of the election) :

With regard even to the use I shall make of creatures, these great thoughts, these lofty thoughts of the children of God, will help me to remain free of any self-seeking. I want to see them as God's work, His creatures, His friends, His instruments, the images and messengers of His love; to love them in God, that is, want them to have the enduring Good and the supreme Love; to seek their help and help them in the acquisition of this Good; to realize that outside this divine perspective I harm them and they harm me. I shall accept without anxious introspection the joys or sorrows that come to me through them, in my labors and friendships, but I will purify this joy and sanctify these sufferings by frequent recourse to God, protesting that I am and remain abandoned in His paternal hands, not only because I have to, but by free choice and out of love, and that I thus embrace in advance all the dispositions of His free and sovereign Providence, begging it to make me, through them, conformable to the only-begotten Son and supreme

Exemplar of all divine sonship in this world, and of all glory given to God by man. May suffering and work make me resemble Jesus on earth, and may my soul be inwardly conformed by grace to His soul, the soul of a Son, an Apostle, and a Friend of men. [8]

And here is Father Lebreton's commentary:

A final word dispels the last-mentioned fears: the grace of God. Man cannot hope through his own strength to live such a life of self-sacrifice and of freedom from all human affection. But the grace of God can lead him to it. What is impossible to man is possible to God.

And now the religious clearly sees the goal toward which he is striving, the Master who is leading him, and the strength that impels him. The last meditations of his retreat were to give him still more light and confidence. [9]

Children of God and disciples of Jesus

The problem we are considering in the footsteps of Father de Grandmaison is germane to every Christian life. It must be frankly faced by present-day Christians who are aware of the imperatives of their faith. The elite among believers make exacting demands. They will not accept sham. They want no part of a narrow Christianity that allows the believer to neglect his various obligations as a man. Nor do they want an edulcorated Christianity. They insist on living a Christianity in tune with the needs and aspirations of its own time, and yet not a bargain-basement religion. And this problem which the Christian elite clearly understands concerns all believers.

Christian humanism is not merely reverence for the human spirit. Christian social action is something more than a program for personality development. Christian marriage is far more than a marriage that rises above the level of vulgar satisfaction. Christian education involves much more than a profound human

[8] J. LEBRETON, *op. cit.*, p. 132.
[9] *Ibid.*

fulfillment. The dialectics of commitment and detachment must be an essential part of it. The mark of Christian humanism is that it includes both a real death to the human and a genuine interest in every man. The Christian social movement can promote the cause of the working class only by deepening poverty of spirit among those who benefit from better working conditions. The believer can pursue the Christian ideal of marriage only if his love of God transcends his love for his spouse. Christian education deserves the name only if it trains the child to cultivate all these Christian attitudes.

Now the attainment of such an impossible equilibrium will remain utopian unless we seek not equilibrium but fidelity to the living God. Psychologically it is a very different thing to ask ourselves if a given attitude is good or bad, or to ask ourselves if it conforms to the call of God who loves us and to whom we are consecrated. But we must go one step further. We must believe not only in God's call, but also in His grace.

The only way we can be supernaturally committed to earthly tasks and healthily detached from created things is by living in this personal relationship with the God of mercy, by whom we know we are loved, or to put it more concretely, in an attitude of fidelity to Jesus the Redeemer, a fidelity that is a form of prayer.

If we are content to profess an abstract morality, and thus to rank God's law above God Himself, we may well discover principles of humanism and social progress in Christian doctrine. But we shall not find the absolutely unique elements of Christian humanism or of the social teaching of the Church.

Marxist doctrine has many enticing aspects, and Jehovah's Witnesses are very dynamic, but the uniqueness of Christianity lies in the fact that Christians find salvation in a love, and are impelled by love. We are not merely defenders of an ideology, we are men who love with all our hearts. This is what makes us see everything in a different light, this is why we are at once deeply committed and yet detached, interested in earthly realities and yet emancipated from all passing things.

We need to understand that God deserves to be loved; and that we must propagate esteem for God, a spirit of adoration and prayer that will give an evangelical character to all Christian

morality, especially to the Christian concepts of work and of
marriage.

We are not merely exponents of a theory of man, of moral
principles, or of a philosophy of the human spirit. First and
above all we are children of the Father, and disciples of Jesus.
The Savior lives our life within us; and we live our life with
Him. In our midst and within each of us is the presence of the
risen Christ. We have placed our faith in Him, and our hope as
well. We have received the following message from His own
lips: the first law is that the observance of law and the defense of
truth must come from the heart. The first law is to love God
with all our heart, and soul, and strength. We must love our God,
and be transmitters of His grace so that He may be more widely
loved. Then only will we observe the other commandments
as we ought.

Our God is Someone. That is the essential. We cannot
solve our problems with ideas and acts of the will. We cannot
be authentic Christians, uncompromisingly and yet without
bigotry, except through union with Jesus.

When a marriage is well-knit, each of the spouses sees much
more clearly, for example, how much attachment and detachment
he should have with regard to material goods. The union
between a man and his wife is made up in great part of a spirit
of generous and well-balanced poverty. If, on the other hand,
there is discord between them, then they will be less completely
emancipated from attachments to material things. As a result,
the effort to achieve detachment will be much harder and lack
moral vigor.

This is true of Christian life as a whole. Only our personal
union with God present in our lives will enable us to be in the
world without being of the world. We must live with Christ
who died and rose again, rejoicing in the mercy God has shown
us, and abandoning ourselves to grace without ignoring its
demands or doubting that it will help us.

It is impossible to take a sane view of how much we should
concede to nature and how much we must refuse it unless we
remain in the climate of union with God through prayer. For
without this union, abstract metaphysical or psychological
considerations will be deceiving. We must be caught up in the

supernatural order if we would understand in a true and concrete way that grace, which, while it does not abolish nature, requires it to die and gives it a share in the resurrection.

How can we follow a spiritual itinerary similar to that of Father de Grandmaison? We will be on the right road if we accept Christian faith, cling to the hope brought by Christ, and submit to the Commandments, the first of which is to love. This is the course of the theological life, as demanded by supernatural love. Even the crudest faith, if it is genuine, is of the same nature as the contact with God experienced by the mystics. Thus even the smallest degree of charity is akin, if it is truly alive, to the love of the Only One professed by the greatest saints. God does not ask all believers to attain the same high state, but He asks all of them to take the same road, to advance in the same direction.

The vocation of all believers is to know God and to love Him, to be loyal to the God of holiness in the person of Jesus, and in the footsteps of Jesus. We shall all be tempted to stop at Jesus' message, without being captivated by Jesus Himself; to want to be men of principle instead of men whom Jesus loves and who love Him in return. If we dedicate our life to a cause instead of surrendering ourselves to Someone, we shall be professing a concept of man and an ideal of individual or collective progress that will not differ substantially from philosophical systems built on metaphysical principles. We shall no longer be in the realm of the supernatural or clearly understand how to reconcile commitment and detachment. On the other hand, if we allow faith, hope, and charity to fill our souls, and let ourselves be possessed by the God who makes us die and live, we shall be recognizing Father de Grandmaison's problem as our very own, as the problem of every Christian.

There is a basic identity in the call received by the lowliest Christian eking out his existence in the world and the most perfect religious belonging to the most austere Order. God may ask of some who, like Father de Grandmaison, have a taste for letters, science, teaching, and spiritual direction, to renounce all these things in practice and bury themselves in the silence of a monastery. He may ask others to remain in the world as laymen. There are men who will never in their entire lives have the capacity that Father de Grandmaison had in a single day for placing himself in the Lord's presence. But He will ask each one, according to his own lights and to the particular indications of Providence, to judge and act with the same fundamental docility to grace.

All Christians are asked to live supernaturally and to give themselves to Christ, to follow the inspiration of the first disciples who recognized Him, even at the beginning of His public life, as the dispenser of the true life. They are asked to continue in their own lives the conversion of those who, after Pentecost, believed in His Resurrection and in His living presence in the Christian community as it moves onward toward the eternal community of heaven.

Living the life of the risen Jesus:
  commitment and detachment inspired by charity born of prayer

To live supernaturally by the life of the risen Christ is to live by grace in the climate of supernatural charity. It is to live theologically, and to love the God of Abraham, Isaac, and Jacob, the God of Jesus Christ. What is demanded of every Christian above all else is a love founded on faith and prolonged in hope. But this fundamental attitude is the fruit of a grace that we must dare to take seriously and with which we must cooperate through prayer: the humble prayer of the pauper who knows his Father's heart and acknowledges his own indigence. The core of every Christian soul must be Mary's *fiat*.

These, then, are the conclusions to which we are led by our study of Father de Grandmaison's texts and our own expatiation on the demands of the supernatural vocation. The elementary truths are as follows. The theological life is the answer to the problem of the relative importance we must give to the tasks of the world on the one hand and to detachment from the world on the other. The soul must be quickened by charity, and charity must be nourished by prayer. The God whom we worship asks us to answer His love by our faith, and hence to fall on our knees.

Without these dispositions, we may still accomplish great things. But that is not what really matters. What is important is that God accomplish great things in us. That will demand action of us, but action accomplished in complete surrender to Him. And that is the beginning here on earth of the eternal life of the risen.

Our hearts must cleave to God so that He may work in them and guide them. Then what is humanly impossible will come to pass. We shall discern His Will for us and acquire the capacity to cooperate with it. And this grace is offered to every Christian.

PART FOUR

CONVERTING DEFEAT INTO VICTORY

VII   The problem of suffering

The religious problem

The problem that faces man most persistently and acutely is probably the problem of the attitude he should take toward suffering. Two types of solution present themselves: one is technical in nature, and the other relates to the interior life.

Solutions of the first sort consist in suppressing evil as completely as possible. They come to us in part through the sciences that help us to better understand and use the material world and the human body. But these are only partial and temporary solutions. The advances of medical science will never render superfluous the art of self-mastery and the fortitude to suffer nobly. Even in a world that is perfectly organized scientifically speaking, there will still be accidents, sickness, and death. Man will still question the human value of suffering, and he will still need a doctrine that gives misfortune meaning.

A scientific approach to suffering does not dispense us from seeking an interpretation of it that will satisfy the heart and soul. The philosopher must deal with the problem of evil, and every philosophy gives an important place to the origins of suffering and to its role. For those who admit the existence of one or more deities ruling the world, the question of how to react to trials is subordinate to another, namely: for what purpose does the Superior Being upon whom man depends send, or at least allow, trials?

The problem of suffering, therefore, is one that must be faced by every religion. Most religions are based upon an interpretation of suffering, and the most primitive religions are simply means of setting in motion invisible forces to conjure suffering.

The problem of suffering has a particular cogency for the man who entertains the concept of a God who is at once good and all-powerful, and it is under this aspect that the Christian must face it. It can be said that Christianity is essentially an answer to this fundamental problem. Its Founder is the Man of Sorrows, the Crucified risen from the dead, the great Sufferer whose anguish brought Him to the right hand of the Father. His doctrine joins beatitude with death to self, His life offers a program of action, He wants us to follow Him through trials to glory. His salvific work consists in opening up the way so we can follow Him. Christianity presents suffering to us as the consequence of sin. It sees acceptance of suffering as the means of conquering sin, thanks to the sacrifice of Christ, and even of conquering suffering itself, which has now become a tool for the moral ascent of the sinner.

Before considering this Christian solution, let us take a rapid glance at what we can expect of reason on the one hand, and of faith on the other.

Reason and faith

Our sufferings would constitute a serious objection against the God of the Christians if they made the concept of this God contradictory, i.e., if there were an evident incompatibility between divine goodness and the trials that befall man. Obviously we cannot appeal to the evidence in this matter. Moreover it is not the evidence that shocks us but a lack of clarity. It is the word " Why? " that stops us in our tracks. This question is forced upon us, and it apparently has no human answer.

Insoluble: this is the way the problem of human suffering often appears to reason. And if our faith does not deceive us, this is the way it appears to our belief. There is no answer to the questions arising from God's way of dealing with our world, committed to a supernatural destiny, except within the context of the mystery of the Redemption.

Philosophy can certainly enlighten us, but it cannot satisfy those of us who have faith. In fact it cannot suffice for anyone, since human life is lived in a context of divine initiatives that stem from a gratuitous love unforeseeable to the philosopher. The scandal of suffering cannot be ended for the unbeliever by making the world intelligible to him and dispensing him from religious belief. He must, on the contrary, be shown the aspects of the Christian faith which he forgets when he is scandalized by suffering. If he is to grasp the meaning of his life, the God of faith must be revealed to him, and not merely the Prime Mover that he can discover through his intellect. If human reason, left to itself, is incapable of reconciling God's goodness and the defects of the created world, if faith alone can pacify the soul made uneasy by the fact of suffering, it is far more an argument for believing than an objection to belief.

For the Christian, it would be a strange procedure to explain suffering without reference to Christ, or to try to justify God outside the perspectives of sin and the Redemption. And yet are we not easily tempted to do so? We lose sight of the fact that the concrete order in which we live calls us to the supernatural life. We reason, forgetting that we have faith, a faith that is not merely belief in the existence of a God but the acceptance of a Revelation. It is in this Revelation that we must seek the meaning of the present state of the world.

Understanding Someone

Only an act of faith can enable us to accept an answer to suffering that appeals to the supreme Christian mystery—the mystery of sin and of Redemption. Acceptance of Christianity's solution to the problem of suffering puts an end to the revolt born of inability to find a solution. But it does not put an end to the mystery of suffering. It is not faith's function to make known a doctrine that is self-justifying once it is manifested, making the act of faith useless.

But even without elucidating the mystery implicit in the necessity of suffering, Christian doctrine allows us to make God's views more completely our own. Knowing a mathematical theorem is very different from knowing someone. Understanding someone is compatible with mystery, and it can even grow with keener awareness of the mystery. We understand our brothers better in the measure that we see them as personal beings, profoundly different from things, endowed with an innate richness that God alone can fathom. This is true likewise of our knowledge of God. The more we see Him not only as the First Cause indispensable to an explanation of the world, but as Someone who loves us in a splendid and mysterious way that is His privilege alone, the better we shall understand His actions. And this not so much because we gave greater insight into His motives as because our souls are more perfectly in harmony with Him.

Reason can enable us to guess what is in God's heart. It can prepare the way to the acceptance of a God who is Love, and who —for a purpose that is necessarily mysterious to us—permits suffering while giving us the opportunity to make a treasure out of it. However, the argument of reason is infinitely less compelling than the Revelation of God Himself.

Scholarly knowledge is a help to a better understanding of the " living God, " but it is infinitely more helpful to resemble Him. The Christian solution to the problem of suffering is not a scholarly solution; nor is it a sentimental one. In order to grasp it we need not merely a keen intellect or superficial emotion, but a deep capacity for understanding that springs from our entire personality. To accept the fact of suffering demands more than a way of thinking or feeling. It calls for a way of being and living.

That is why we learn to accept suffering less through argumentation than through contagion of spirit. To make others understand the Lord, we must be akin to Him; to make others accept the God of love who permits suffering we must, even as we love Him, understand and love those who suffer. We cannot get anyone to admit the existence of the Christian God except by making him love Him. And we can educate others to love only in the measure that we love both those we want to educate and the One we are offering to their love.

True, suffering is not the whole problem of God. The soundness of Chritianity's solution to the problem of suffering is not the only point to be considered in evaluating the foundations of our Faith. But we are not dealing with these more general questions here. Suffice it to note that neither the unbeliever who wants to understand the Christian interpretation of the world nor the believer baffled by the problem of suffering will be able to take on the spirit of Christ except at the price of total self-surrender.

Suffering with and for Someone

Every judgment on the events that happen in this world must be based on a scale of values. If we want to understand anything of God's work, therefore, it is important to realize what is essential in His eyes—i.e., what is essential in itself, and not according to our own momentary impression. The values that God has in view in His creation are moral values. Compared with these, all other values are but means for Him, as they should be for us. Even philosophy can convince us, just as experience proves concretely, that trials are often the source of riches. Triumphs of the spirit are worth as much as they cost us. Suffering requires an effort on our part that we would not have had the strength to demand of ourselves if we were not suffering. Many souls owe their spiritual ascent to suffering. It can even be said that suffering is irreplaceable and that one can almost always single out those whom it has purified.

The Gospel confirms and extends the conclusions of reason. Christ has reminded us that there is no worse misfortune than to lose our soul, and that we can save it only by renouncing everything else. He has given Himself to us as an exemplar. He gave us the means of hearing and following Him. He suffered so that we might live His sufferings in our own, so that we might have the opportunity to make a fulcrum out of our misfortunes.

Christianity attributes value to suffering, and thus gives us what we need most when we suffer. It detaches us from ourselves by restoring our motives for living and acting, that is, for self-giving. Despondency is inability to make an effort. We are saved from it if we rediscover reasons for willing that can survive our anguish. And even our anguish can take on value when it becomes the object of self-giving. The Christian has the privilege of never being without something to offer and without someone to love.

Even as Christianity raises our spirits by restoring our sense of purpose amid trials, it revives our confidence. Christ suffered so that we might be able to imitate Him. We can and must share His victory over suffering and death.

But why such a high price and why so much waste?

If suffering thus accepted takes on meaning, this meaning justifies the One who permits suffering. But may we not wonder why God allows our moral victories to be so costly? Besides, it is not our trials themselves that elevate us, but the way we accept them. For by its very nature suffering can kill quite as well as vivify. And in fact while many souls are purified by suffering, many others are broken by it. Why does God tolerate the suffering of children utterly unable to give any value to their pain? Why does He permit so many adults, by reason of the conditions under which they suffer (notably defects in their heredity or their education) to be incapable of making the most of their sufferings, or even of avoiding the degradation that often comes with suffering? Why so much wasted pain, so much harmful pain? The moral triumphs born of suffering seem so few compared to the defeats of all sorts it entails. Who can explain why God has recourse to means of elevating man that involve so much waste?

True, we are poor judges of this waste. We know so little about the secret of men's consciences that we have no way of guessing God's verdict at the moment their eternity is decided. And yet it is a truth of faith that some lives can end in irremediable disaster, for the existence of hell is a dogma. How can we admit that God who is Knowledge and Love should be the author of a world in which evil, and such virulent evil, is so intimately intermingled with good?

Reason can answer that only an infinitely good God can be at the origin of all created goods, and that this certitude must prevail over any doubts resulting from our encounter with evil. This is a sound answer, but if we limit ourselves to the conclusions of reason, our certitude is merely the result of intricate philosophical arguments. A cold-blooded observation of the baffling facts, on the other hand, seems to revive doubt.

It is legitimate to point out here that the quality of God's work is not to be judged by statistics. God does not give heaven to us ready-made. He expects us to make it ourselves, and this is admirable of Him. The success of the elect who have made their choice in favor of God amid struggles and dangers is sufficient reason for the creation of our world of struggle, danger, and defeat, even if there seem to be more defeats than victories. It may be objected that God is not obliged, as we are, to pay a price for the good He has in view. That is very true. But there is no contradiction in His permitting defeats due entirely to the freedom of His creatures, all of whom without exception He wants to save.

But can these considerations drive all anxiety from our minds and hearts? If these thoughts are to have their maximum impact on us, we must reflect on them humbly, with the respect for mystery required of anyone who places himself in God's presence. We must not try to understand God's ways as if we were dealing with a problem of physics. Man may not approach the Lord as if He were just one of his fellow men. This is not only a moral imperative, it is an imperative of the intellect as well.

Before the crucifix

Without the support of Revelation, the human mind finds it hard to understand God. But what God Himself tells us of His transcendence and of His way of loving makes possible for the man of good will something that is almost impossible for the philosopher who depends only on his reason. The simple believer can in a certain sense guess the Divine Personality, and convince himself concretely, by becoming acquainted with God's ways, of the total trust our Father in heaven deserves.

Revelation shows us the Lord at work. It tells us where He wants to lead us, how He reacts to our needs and punishes our revolts. At the root of evil, Revelation points to sin. Obviously our involvement in original sin and its consequences plunges us deep into mystery, but it ends with our participation in Christ's victory over sin and over its consequences, suffering and death. The God that Christianity reveals to us is a God whose every act fills us with assurance. This is true above all of the way He has made our trials His own in the person of His Son.

We can rely on a God who has entered so completely into the drama of human suffering. We can be sure of Someone who loves the way Christ has loved us. We can face the problem of the suffering of innocents when we look up at Christ, Innocence itself, on the Cross. We can put our trust unreservedly in the One who has freely chosen death on Calvary in order to save men in their bitter struggle against themselves and against the forces that oppress them. Can anyone bear rancor against a Man crucified in pure self-giving? Can we doubt the mercy of the One who led Him to Golgotha? Before the crucifix, the Christian rediscovers peace. He understands God better, even if he does not grasp His reasons! He finds an answer to his "Why's." It is not the answer one would expect to find in a semester examination; it is the answer a puzzled child expects of his father. It is a source of trust rather than a justification.

Suffering can remain an invincible difficulty for those who do not have faith. The Christian, on the contrary, knows enough about his God to justify the confidence he places in Him. It is the God of the Christians whom we must defend when the objection of evil is thrown up to us, and not merely the conclusions of philosophy. We can show that the intellect does not possess the premises that would allow it to conclude against God, that it leads only to an absence of any totally satisfying solution. Then we can show that Christianity brings an answer to the problem that militates in favor of God's veracity. But the Christian answer to the problem of suffering, if it is to be accepted, requires a receptive soul, capable of trust so that it can be taught, and capable of arousing trust in others.

Jesus has triumphed over suffering

Christ's message teaches the necessity of suffering, and at the same time it is a message of joy. The earliest Christian writings were cries of victory amid the despair or gloomy resignation of the pagans. Christ has overcome suffering as well as sin, and He wants us to share in His triumph. We shall soon be united to the eternal glorification of the suffering Christ. Today, made lucid and strong by faith, hope, and charity, let us join Christ, as sons of God through His Passion, in accepting the Will of the Father.

VIII Divine fatherhood
and redemptive suffering

A mystery of justice or a mystery of love?

God could have spared us suffering. He preferred to share it with us. The central mystery of our faith is the mystery of God made man, of the eternal Son become a son of Adam, and being subjected with us to the consequences of sin, in order to make us emerge from the world of sin into the universe of sanctity.

When we think of sin and of the Redemption, should we picture an intractable God who vented His anger on the One who consented to take our place? When we speak of the Passion, are we to see in it a conflict between divine love and a need for divine justice which prevailed over every other consideration? Scripture forbids us to do so. It was the God of love who consented, because He was Love, to the sacrifice of Calvary. And yet Scripture also says that Jesus, the " blessed one, " made Himself accursed with the accursed, that He paid our ransom. St. Paul uses very strong words when he discusses God's demands for our redemption.

We find God's views evoked by Isaias' description of the persecuted just man and by the texts of the New Testament concerning the sacrifice of Christ. In order to gain some insight into these views, we must rise above our spontaneous and almost instinctive ways of thinking. We must appeal to that portion of our human experience that belongs most completely to the life of the spirit.

Is God impassible?

First of all, how can we speak at one and the same time of God's impassibility and of His way of being affected by our sins and our misfortunes? There are two kinds of impassibility. One comes from interior poverty, and the other proceeds from richness of spirit. The first is the impassibility of inert matter, and that of the spiritual being still close to matter. The second is revealed to us by the saints. It has nothing in common with indifference, it is not a lack of sensibility. A saint feels the misery of his fellows more than others do. He understands it, experiences it, makes it truly his own. He is not content to be compassionate from the side lines. He lives it together with the unfortunate. Suffering does not merely arouse a flood of good will in him, it stirs him to the depths of his soul. And yet it does not cause him to lose his serenity. His sharing in the misery of his fellows does not impair his own soul. He is at once more deeply affected and less disturbed than we are.

Let us press our analogy to its utmost limit, following a procedure commonly used by mathematicians. We shall then be able to describe the attitude of the saints in heaven. They are united to us in our tribulations not as spectators but far more deeply than our dearest friends and than those most advanced in perfection here on earth. And yet they do not cease to be in the state of beatitude. Similarly we can form a feeble idea of our God's attitude toward us. He is in possession of happiness that nothing can impair, and yet all of His interventions in the history of salvation show how deeply our fate touches Him in His innermost Being. We might call to mind the biblical expressions that describe His obstinate love, His passionate pursuit of man fleeing His grace. We might reread His laments and cries of anguish in the Book of Revelation.

God is inexpressibly touched by everything that touches us. He is deeply moved by the adventure in which we are engaged, and infinitely more so than any of those who love us on earth and in heaven. And at the same time He is Joy that nothing can darken in any way. He has done more for us than any of those who have given us their affection, He went unhesitatingly and without repentance to the end of the sacrifice of Calvary. And

He was not merely acting " as if, " He did not merely adopt
without emotion attitudes He would have taken if misfortune had
touched Him! His actions proved He was not looking at our
suffering as a stranger. It is unthinkable that His attitudes were
merely external, and that deep within Himself He was not affected
by our destiny. And yet at the very moment the Son of God was
dying on the Cross, God did not cease to be God, the God of
eternal happiness. He was, He is, and He will always be the One
who lacks nothing; and nevertheless He felt the lack of us so
poignantly that He gave us His Son. Eternally He is plenitude,
the One who can know neither change nor diminution nor increase,
and He is the One who missed us so much that He was willing to
use the most extreme means to bring us back to Himself.

Divine selflessness in the Redemption

Closely related to the question of God's impassibility is the
doctrine concerning the selflessness of His action. Let us
approach it from the point of view we took in dealing with the
paradoxical situation of God in the face of suffering.

When we want to save someone, our desire to help him is
secretly infiltrated with a need for achievement. After we have
gone to the aid of others, we are not only happy to know their
misery has been relieved, we are also happy to have accomplished
something, we are pleased with ourselves. We find fulfillment
in carrying out an exterior work. What we do helps us as well as
our neighbor, and our unselfishness easily degenerates. Self-
seeking creeps into even the most generous initiatives of charity.

The saint is far better able than we to take an interest in
others for their own sakes. This is clearly revealed when, for
example, he encounters ingratitude or defeat. In such circumstances we are likely to be discouraged. The man or woman who
is more completely emancipated from egoism has less need to see
the results of his effort. He is less subject to discouragement, and
less discountenanced if those he has helped forget what they owe
him once they are prosperous.

Let us again carry this analogy to the limit in speaking of
God. In the Redemption He has done the improbable to save us,

and yet He has no need of us in order to be Himself. He has nothing to gain by rehabilitating us. We must not look upon the Redemption as though it were a victory by which God finally obtained redress for the wrongs done Him. We must insist on God's mysterious selflessness, and show that in this undertaking we are the sole benefactors, that it involves incomparably more generosity than any imaginable human philanthropy. God does not depend on His creatures for His happiness. He is incommensurable with us in every way, above anything we may think or feel in His regard. He gratuitously does infinitely more good than the holiest of men. While He is more compassionate of our misfortunes than anyone, He is absolutely independent of them. He expects no enrichment from our salvation; and He loves us as no one else can, simply for ourselves.

God's understanding of sin

We have been dealing with suffering primarily in terms of the paradoxes implicit in the encounter between God's transcendence and fallen man. Let us now reflect on sin, considering once more the difference between instinctive attitudes and the attitudes of the saints. This will help us to understand a little better the One who alone is the Holy One.

Let us picture the reactions of a crowd on the occasion of an assassination. When the criminal goes by, the mob runs wild. In its indignation at this man's crime, it clamors for his death. It demands severe punishment. And yet it sees this crime as scarcely more than an attack against a biological life. It has only a very confused sense of the seriousness of the murder of an innocent person. It has not grasped how this act is an attack against the essential laws of morality; or how it degrades, as a human being, the man who has become an assassin. The proof lies in the fact that it would not be so indignant over an abortion! Basically impelled by the instinct for self-preservation, the crowd feels the need to assure its own security by punishing assassination in an exemplary way. Its reactions are inspired less by the desire to defend law and order than by fear. It is profoundly selfish.

Then a saint passes by. He has a deeper insight than anyone into the heinousness of the murderer's sin; he penetrates much more clearly into the meaning of the moral disorder implicit in homicide. He is more profoundly moved by it than anyone, but in a quiet manner. He is much more indignant, but in a different way. His horror does not drive him to violence. He too wants the criminal to be punished, but he wants it in such a different way. He does not think of himself, but of his brothers—and among these, he thinks of the criminal as well as of the victim, he thinks of Christ, he thinks of God.

Let us raise our thoughts to the Author of all holiness. He alone really understands the malice of sin, He alone is in a position to see the virulence of the disorder. The saint realizes better than anyone, and obviously much better than the assassin himself, the terrible human significance of the criminal act. God measures infinitely better than we the atrocity of our sins. No one else can adequately understand them. And God, whose inspired word tells us of His vast indignation against sin, none the less reacts to this terrible reality far more indulgently than any mortal being could. For, as the Prophet Osee says in His name, He is God and not man, He is the Holy One (cf. Osee 11: 9).

God's understanding of the sinner

Just as God alone can know what sin is, so He alone can understand the sinner. Let us review the instinctive reactions aroused by the sight of an assassin. The crowd's anger can easily give way to sympathy. For example, public opinion has often been on the side of a woman who murdered her husband because he had martyrized her. Lawyers are adept, in criminal court, in appealing to the emotions of the jury. They often conjure up the unhappy childhood of the defendant or the tragedy his conviction will mean for his family. Spectators are thus divided between a desire for vengeance and an impulse to weep over the fate of the criminal. If there happens to be a saint among them who knows the defendant well, he will see things in their true light and also have a more intransigent attitude.

There is a difference between spoiling children and loving them. Those who spoil children—and these are often grand-parents, uncles, aunts, or friends, rather than the parents themselves—are inclined to senseless excessess of affection alternating with inordinate bursts of anger. The reason is that the act of spoiling stems more from instinct than from the life of the spirit. Authentic love makes a person at once more gentle and more demanding; it inspires the lover to educate the one loved. Those who spoil children are motivated by egoism. They are really seeking their own satisfaction when they cajole them, and they draw back in the face of the hard work implicit in genuine education. When a person really loves a child, he has a far deeper insight into the child's faults and takes the necessary steps to correct them.

Most of us try to strike a balance between leniency and severity, and are always swinging over too far in one direction or in the other. We are not as strict as we should be because we do not love enough. If we loved more, we would discover the art of being more demanding without being harsh. When a man progresses in holiness, he advances both in the virtue of charity and in the virtue of justice.

Once again let us push the analogy to the limit and see how it applies to God. God is unreservedly merciful. His under-standing of the sinner is not obscured by any trace of egoism. He alone is good, and He alone is just. In fact, He is supremely good, to the point of being supremely just. Since He is absolutely free of egoism, He can unhesitatingly demand justice. He is the only perfect educator, and the only judge generous enough to be free of weakness. His reaction to sin is a mysterious combination of benevolence and punishment. His love for the sinner is so powerful that it is without affectation or false indulgence, and yet it is more tender than any earthly love. Scripture describes a paradoxical God to us. He cannot be measured by our human standards. His will to save us is infinitely more sincere and absolute than any desire we can have to help our brothers. That is why He is a terrible God, as well as a God of mercy.

A comparison

Let us look at the work of the Redemption in a more concrete way, beginning with an example from human experience. If someone has squandered money we have lent him and become insolvent as a result of his unsavory behavior, we can be generous and forget his debt. But we can be much more generous than that. We can lend him more money to help him regain solvency, demanding in return that he live frugally as befits his indebted condition. We can continue to encourage him and stand by him in this course of action until he has been rehabilitated. We shall then be practicing generosity to the point of satisfying the demands of justice. That is how God has acted with us. He has given us His Son, so that in Him our debt might be paid. Only Christ, the God-man, is in a position to assume with complete adequacy the condition of the sinner; He alone knows what sin is, and can make the reparation to God that sin demands.

Let us not get into any of the arguments that have divided the theological schools on the nature of Christ's merits. Each of the positions taken has its convincing aspects and its weak points. God's justice still remains a mystery, differing as much from our justice as His mercy differs from ours. Obviously we must realize that the work of the Redemption is not in any sense the slaking of a thirst for vengeance on a carefully selected victim who alone is qualified to appease God's anger against the whole human race. God's mercy is not incompatible with severity, but on the contrary requires it. For God acts not through instinctive impulse, but as Pure Spirit.

The Father and the death of the Son-made-man

So far we have been speaking in general terms about God's attitude toward the sins of men. Let us now delve more deeply into the mystery of the Redemption, with respect to the relationship between the Father and the Son-made-man.

It is no innovation to say that the Father did not will the death of Christ, but merely tolerated it. Early Christian writers have stressed this point. In fact, the same can be said of all suffering and death. God resigned Himself in a certain way to this form of punishment for sin, but it was man who willed it by the very nature of his act. Moreover God consented to this punishment for the race of Adam only with foreknowledge of what the Word Incarnate would accomplish through death. God knew what form the Redemption would take when He punished original sin. He promised to reinstate man at the very moment He punished him. And conversely, He had the Incarnation in mind when He created the world.

Now if human death is Adam's work rather than God's, the death of Christ on the Cross is even more the work of men. It was the Jews—and all those to whom they were united in a cruel civilization—who drove Him to this extremity. And with them, all men of all times who have become the victims and accomplices of Satan. When our Savior chose to join our sinful family in order to rehabilitate us, He accepted all the risks inherent in this venture. He knew where it would lead Him, and He was moving toward the Cross from the moment of His Incarnation. Such was the Father's Will. While He did not will His Son's death directly, He consented to it in view of what man was, and realizing what a refusal to give man a Messias would mean.

We have been expressing ourselves very clumsily. God is outside time, and to say that He knew in advance what was to happen is scarcely apt. On the other hand, God is no mere spectator, even a very perceptive one, who foresees events before they come to pass. The mystery of predestination is more than the mystery of God's omniscience. The point we want to make is that the Father did not condemn the Son to death. This was the work of men. And yet when the Son accepted death, He was not simply accepting the decision of men, He was submitting to the Will of His Father.

Obedient to death, Jesus redeemed the world by the Cross. That is the path by which He gained access to the Resurrection, both His and ours. He liberated us by a bloody sacrifice, thereby expiating our sins. And this is no contradiction of the Father's love for the Son, or of divine mercy toward the human race in whose name Jesus made expiation. There is no question here of vengeance, but of a love so far above human love that we

cannot find any replica of it in any human work, or grasp all
of its aspects.

Our attitude as forgiven sinners

These are the things to be stressed in considering the mystery
of the Redemption. Let us avoid language that is too exclusively
juridical, that would not awaken a sense of mystery but merely
imply the settling of a debt in the customary way. Let us also
avoid expressions that would imply that in the Redemption
God established a rigorous bookkeeper's balance between the
sufferings of Christ and the sins to be expiated. We must avoid
interposing a sort of bloody decree between the Father and the
Son which would scandalize fatherly love and fail to awaken
filial devotion. In dealing with the superhuman, let us not
become inhuman.

We must never forget that the Father gained no advantage
from Christ's death. It is we who gained everything from it.
There is no common measure between the selflessness, generosity,
and salvific will of both the Father and the Son and the most
complete and purified human self-giving. We must carry to the
extreme limit all that we can know here on earth of absolute
horror for sin and of absolute love for the sinner. We must
become aware of our own smallness and of our meager grasp of
this mystery of salvific love. Let us go to the God of our
Redemption with a humility that enables us to accept our indigence
and shows us our rightful place. Let us adore the God of
holiness as forgiven sinners.

CONCLUSIONS

IX How the Redemption revolutionized the world

Between a merciful past and a future it has made secure

We live between a past filled with mercy and a future made secure by this past. Each divine fulfillment is a step forward in a march that nothing can stop. The works accomplished in the Old Testament were presages of what the New Covenant would bring. The New Testament in turn was only a start. It opened the era of salvation that will be consummated in heaven. We have wonderful events behind us, and the most amazing is still to come. We are sustained at once by thanksgiving and expectation. We live as children of the Father, joining gratitude to petition in our prayer, each inspiring the other.

When Christ walked on our earth, the world went through a decisive stage. We now live in an age when the kingdom has been established. We are members of the new Israel, of the new holy people. How has the world been changed by the Redemption?

Externally, it is exactly the same as before. Some day the face of all things will be transformed. Even matter will share in the new life of the spirit. It will be the consummation of the Redemption in the general resurrection, the total kingship of Christ over bodies as well as souls.

Today this transformation is still inward. Christ has taken possession of the depths of our souls, a fact that neither we nor our wayfaring brothers seem to fully realize. Our true self is hidden from each of us. We cannot see it any more than we can see our own face; and those who see us can only surmise what

we are deep within. Authentic realities are invisible. Faith is
the only means of penetrating them.

We have become children of the Father, together with
the Lord Jesus. But, sons of men that we are, we continue to
fail in our efforts or succeed, suffer or avoid suffering, according
to our human means. The Redemption has not changed these
human means, except as a consequence. The work of Christ
has not modified the law of work and of suffering, except by
changing man and thus changing the purpose of his labors and
of his struggle to survive. Christ has made no change in our
power over inert things and circumstances, over the external
realities on which we depend day after day. But He has taught us
how we should behave in relation to them, and Christian morality
has certainly influenced the evolution of civilization since Jesus of
Nazareth appeared on this earth. The visible course of events
thus reflects slightly, but only slightly, the invisible change that
grace produces in men's hearts.

There is something deeper and more hidden. The work of
Redemption proceeds at a depth that no one can fathom and that
we shall completely understand only in heaven. Defeat and
success, suffering and happiness have taken on a new meaning
that we cannot know now except by supernatural knowledge,
through the instrumentality of the theological virtues. The most
far-reaching transformation accomplished by the Redemption
can be seen in its full truth only by those who live by faith, hope,
and charity.

Transforming things devoid of human meaning

First of all, the transformation of suffering. The light and
strength of Christ can greatly limit suffering. Our lives are
poisoned less by inevitable trials like sickness than by the
wounding of our self-love and sensibilities, by incomprehension
and discord. Let us question ourselves and those around us.
The most painful thing in our lives is not illness, for example,
but the hostility that sets us against one another in so many,
ways: political battles, commercial rivalries, social conflicts,
ideological differences, and temperamental incompatibilities.

The world would already be much less cruel if men would stop hurting one another and misjudging their brothers in so many ways. If we were all converted, truly converted, we would escape in great part the punishments bound up with original sin that are daily intensified by our many actual sins. All of us are at once initiators and victims of these conflicts that do so much to mutilate our lives as men.

The Redemption is destined to comfort man by changing his ways, but its action is most powerful at a deeper level. Christ did not merely assume our nature, He became a member of our race and a son of Adam like ourselves. He shared our fate, experienced incomprehension and hostility, even suffering death on a cross. He has known defeat to the point of becoming humanly useless, of hanging on a gibbet where, after the conversion of the good thief, He could find no one to convert by His preaching. Those who had once listened to Him sympathetically now shook their heads from afar, thinking they had been deceived. Even the Apostles were distraught. Now His enemies had the upper hand. As for Himself, His past successes had come to nothing, and He had no future. His temporary achievements now seemed permanently destroyed, and He seemed no longer good for anything, as far as men could see. Christ experienced the crushing of man by man. He also lived through the annihilation in which every life ends, even if it has been a series of successes. He suffered agony and death.

But He changed the deep and invisible significance of these consequences of sin. He gave value to something that has none from the purely human point of view. He triumphed over Satan by turning his own weapons against him. He conquered sin even in its effects. At the very moment of defeat He was the victor, transforming defeat into victory. His ascent to Calvary was at once the last stage of defeat and a triumphal march.

And what Christ has done for Himself has been continued in us. In a Christian life there is no meaningless waste. Once our actions are encompassed by faith, they all become fruitful. Our sufferings build our ultimate happiness, our death is a victory over death and opens eternal life to us. All the negative aspects of our career become positive. The Redemption has " converted " our sufferings, tranfigured them. Whatever crushed us before is now at our mercy. Instead of annihilating us, it becomes a treasure in our hands. If we were really logical, if our thoughts were completely inspired by the spirit of faith, there would be no room for discouragement in our souls.

Christ has traveled the same road as we. He shouldered the burden of our sinful condition, and restored all things. He bears our misfortunes in us and with us, and through His grace things that seem to happen to our detriment really work to our advantage. What is meaningless in the eyes of the world becomes precious in the eyes of God. At the deepest levels of reality, nothing is devoid of meaning for the disciples of the Man who passed by way of death to the Resurrection.

Repercussions on human values

Human values likewise receive new meaning through the Redemption.

The influx of grace into man's soul can and must have an effect on the success of his earthly activities. This is particularly true in the moral order. The Redemption encourages progress in the natural virtues, and Christian civilization is necessarily founded on justice and peace. In the field of material progress as well, Christ's victory has its repercussions. Duty and charity inspire men to take temporal tasks to heart, and guide the believer's practical efforts to achieve a better world.

However, just as the Redemption invisibly transforms things that are meaningless at the purely human level, it also transfigures things that have human meaning in their own right, independently of the supernatural. Our Savior's work, which transfigured our defeats, also changes the aspect of our successes. And this transformation, seen only by the eyes of faith, is the one that really matters.

Human progress, even in the realm of morality, can no longer be what we esteem most in the world. While there is real value in being sound of body and mind, cultured, generous, endowed with a versatile and powerful personality, " somebody " instead of just a " nobody, " capable of exercising control over matter and over self, and of great achievements, all these things

are really very secondary. The primordial thing is to be children
of the Father, and all the rest must be subordinated to the desire
to live as His children. The Church serenely asks all of us to be
children, to have childlike souls. She asks this of the intelligent,
energetic, highly educated man of today, capable of titanic
undertakings, the adult man who invented electricity, radar,
television, jet-engines, and the atom bomb. She quietly proclaims
that initiative and vitality are nothing without the spirit of childhood. For, she says, in God's eyes there is no common measure
between the man of superior endowments, of vigorous intellect
and strongly molded character, but whose heart is closed to
grace because of pride, between this superman on the one hand
and the savage on the other, indigent psychologically as well as
materially, but whose soul is open to the Redemption.

In very truth, Christ came to set everything topsy-turvy,
to give us scales of value that have no place in the world of
reasonableness and earthly wisdom in which we move. When
the world is seen with the eyes of faith, at the deepest level of
reality, its dimensions are completely different. To live according
to Christ, according to truth, according to reality, demands a
complete change of perspective. We must be witnesses to this
invisible reality, appear among our brothers as men whose
eyes perceive something more than the outer shell of things
grasped by the senses or the reason. We must take our stand in
accordance with our spirit of faith.

That means we must live as though dead to ourselves,
by a new life. Ours is the state of those who have risen from
the dead. The Mass, the memorial of Jesus' passage through
death to the life of the Resurrection, the " mystery of faith, "
must bring us back each day to the same perspectives.

X   Docility to our vocation

God is initiative

To live as a Christian is to live with the knowledge that we are loved.

God is not merely Someone who loves. He is love, He is Love in act.

Being Love, God is initiative. Each of our efforts to get closer to Him proceeds from Him. Everything in us that has any value is the fruit of His attraction.

The world was called into existence at His command. The Bible tells us all things came forth and took their proper place in obedience to His voice. His efficacious word called light into being, separated the land and the waters.

Throughout the history of the world and throughout our own lives, God has retained the initiative. He has always been the first to love, and His choices are not commanded by any force that could limit His liberty.

The Christian's progress must consist in a constant co-operation with His gifts, a trusting response to His invitation, an affectionate abandonment to His grace.

An inventive cooperation

The Spirit dwells within us. Renewed by Him, we share in the life of the Trinity. Docile to His inspiration, we dare join with Jesus in saying " Father. "

The Holy Spirit does not dictate to us. He questions

us, calls us, and arouses our responses, without putting Himself in our place.

Christian life is not the execution of a plan that God pre-ordained without us, but the elaboration of an undertaking in which He wants our inventive cooperation.

Providence does not dispense us from providing for the future; divine initiative does not reduce us to passivity; the action of the Almighty does not make our action superfluous.

The mark of our task as men, seen in the light of faith, is not that our progress is led by another in a way that dispenses us from taking a creative attitude. Its uniqueness lies in the fact that this task is to be accomplished in unison with God and with humanity on the march, as a work of love to which we have been invited without having any right to it, without deserving it.

A personal mission

Consider how a father hopes that his son will succeed in a fine career. If this son is outstanding intellectually or through his capacity for action, if he breaks out of a mediocre milieu and attains brilliant social prestige, but if he uses his successes to serve his pride and selfishness, then his disappointed father will say: " I certainly have reason to be proud of him, and yet I was expecting something far better. Here is someone whose knowledge (or qualities of leadership) cannot be denied, but he is not really a son to me. "

A professor may be content to transmit his knowledge to others, a leader may feel satisfied that he has inculcated methods of efficient action, but a father wants something else.

And yet it cannot be said that a father normally has less ambition for his son than a professor or a leader. The father is no less eager for his son's success, but he wants it in a different way.

Now let us look at the son's attitude toward the mission to which he has been invited. He can devote himself to a career recommended by his father, and assume responsibility for it together with his father. That is to conceive and want his career in a different way than if he were choosing it alone; it is to work in a different way than if he were merely following the directives of an instructor.

Thus our Christian faith, in teaching us to say the *Our Father*, makes us see all things in a new light.

God's ambitions in our regard

For us, all problems are posed in personal terms. We think as if we were alone in the world when we ask ourselves if an attitude is reasonable or not, whether it is just or unjust. Even a pagan could look at things that way.

The true Christian way of formulating a question is: Does this attitude conform with the spirit of the Lord; is it in harmony with the Father's call?

There is something more than principles in our lives. There is Someone, Someone who loves us with a deep and demanding familial love. What ambitions does His love have for us?

That is how we should search our souls when we decide on a general course of action, or even on a detail. The transformation of the question in this way will throw penetrating light on the factors involved.

Obviously, in discerning the Father's Will in our regard, we must consider what is reasonable and unreasonable, useful or futile, in line with our aptitudes or contrary to our temperamental endowments. But the ways we think and the conclusions we reach will be greatly modified if we think in union with God rather than by ourselves, with gratitude for God's freely given love rather than with calculations for achieving success, in a spirit of prayer rather than of independence.

In the presence of others

The vocation of each one of us is part of a call issued to all of God's people, to the whole human race.

Our destiny as Christians and our mission as men will be

fulfilled only through collective effort. We are called to share in a common task.

To understand the message the Spirit wants each of us to hear personally, we must take cognizance of the needs and potentialities of others, we must be aware of the wants and aspirations of the milieu with which, willy-nilly, we are inextricably bound up.

No one builds his own life alone, and no one prepares himself for a great work unless he sincerely wants to build with and for others.

Accepting our vocation

When a Christian ponders what career he should choose, he is meditating on his vocation.

He must make his decision in a spirit of prayer, starting out with the thought of God and His fatherly love, and extending his reflection to his neighbor—both proximate and remote—to whom he is united by human and Christian bonds.

This is the climate of thought in which we must question ourselves about our desires, aptitudes, and needs.

The essential is not to become what we would like to be, or what those around us would like us to be, but what God expects us to be. The essential is made clear to us in the petition of the Lord's Prayer: " Thy Will be done. "

If we are going to collaborate in God's Will, we must know what it is, and to this end, we must know our Father's heart. It is with this desire that we must strive to understand ourselves and the world in which we live.

Believing in a great love

A sense of realism demands that we be attentive to both the invisible and the visible, that we have heart as well as reason.

Clarity of vision calls not only for keenness of observation but also for a sense of mystery.

Good judgment presupposes that we are able to trust others.

To see things as they are, we must have the eyes of faith. To understand others and understand ourselves, we must believe in a great love.

To understand God's love, we must be gracious to our neighbor who is the object of this love just as we are.

The mystics are not dreamers, but seers. And if we would escape blindness, we must share in their light.

N. Y. 26 — Printed in Belgium by Desclée & Co, Éditeurs, S. A., Tournai — 10.749